Pleasure

Pleasure

The Secret Ingredient in Happiness

Marisol Garcia, Ph.D.

CONTENTS

FOREWORD

Pleasure has gotten a bad rap in many societies. Engaging in pleasure is believed to be an indulgence that can lead to self-destruction. Images of orgies involving food, drugs and sex come to mind when the word "pleasure" is mentioned. Perhaps pleasure is stigmatized as dangerous because it threatens the need we have to work strenuously. In the United States, we follow Protestant/Puritan teachings of diligence, stringent use of time, sacrifice, and the postponement of pleasure.[1] Enjoyment is deferred until financial stability is achieved.

I propose that we work zealously partly because we have to and partly because we believe that it will provide us with happiness. We believe that diligence, sacrifice and the postponement of pleasure will lead us to success and well-being. Our success and value as a person is determined by hard work, moderation and sacrifice.

What we don't realize is that happiness depends more on how much pleasure we experience than on how much success we achieve. Prominent researchers argue that engaging in pleasurable activities is a crucial component to happiness. They declare that happy people are flourishing human beings and are better off emotionally and physically.[2] Dr. Schindler[1], author of *How to Live 365 Days a Year*, argues that the most common cause of unhappiness is the act of deferring pleasure for the future[3]. Similarly, Maxwell Maltz[2] states that people "do not live, nor do they enjoy life now, but wait for some future event or occurrence."[4]

I was raised between two cultures that have different views on pleasure. My American culture believes that life is best led through stringent management of time, sacrifice, moderation, and austerity. My Dominican culture taught me the exact opposite. In the Dominican, engaging in pleasure is a life long pursuit. Dominicans live to experience pleasure.

I am always amused by the fact that attendance at American social gatherings most often results in discussions regarding what I do for a living, while Dominican social gatherings almost never involve discussions regarding work. I have struggled with these differing views. I knew I could justify working as good

---

[1] John Schindler, M.D. is a best selling author who was one of the first to research and discuss emotionally based illness. His book has been translated into 13 languages.

[2] Maxwell Maltz is the author of the bestselling book, *Psycho-cybernetics*. His book speaks to the importance of having positive self-perception when reaching goals. He argues that goals are impossible to reach unless one changes one's perception of self. In other words, if your goal is to become successful but you believe that you aren't good enough, you will not reach your goals, no matter how hard you work.

for me (to a certain extent) in both cultures, but I couldn't justify engaging in pleasure in the United States.

When I became a therapist and a researcher, I found myself thinking about happiness repeatedly. I wanted to find the best way to help myself and others heal from pain. One day I asked my nine-year-old daughter why it seemed that children were happier than adults. She said it was because children played and adults worked. It was so obvious to her that she added, "Duh, mom."

Her comment incited me to research the connection between pleasure and happiness. I spent three years reading, thinking, discussing, and practicing happiness and pleasure. I found the answers I needed to settle the "battle" I had between pleasure and work.

I learned that a lifestyle focused on pleasure increases physical, mental, emotional, and spiritual well-being. My goal in this book is to provide you with information regarding pleasure and its connection to happiness and to motivate you to expand and enhance your pleasurable experiences so that your sense of well-being and happiness are maximized.[3]

---

[3] Although this book advocates for the engagement in pleasure, I want to be clear that engaging in pleasure is not the only "cure" for unhappiness. No single practice is the cure for anything. Experiencing pleasure is merely one aspect of life that deserves attention.

CHAPTER ONE

The Pleasure in Happiness

We all want to be happy. It doesn't matter where we live or what we do.[5,6,7] Most people would choose happiness over an abundance of money, sex, prestige, or power because without happiness there isn't any sense to having these things. Happiness is our incentive for living. Incentives for living have not changed over time. Aristotle stated that people desire what they desire because they believe it will lead them to happiness.[8]

What Influences Happiness?

The dictionary definition of happiness is "a feeling of well-being and contentment."[9] There are as many ways to define happiness as there are differences in people[4]. Although we may have different definitions as to what happiness is, most of us would say we want more of it. How do we get happiness? Sonja Lyubomirsky, professor at University of California and author of *The How of Happiness* has come up with a happiness model. She has identified three factors responsible for the happiness we experience:[5,10]

- Genetics (50%)
- Context/Circumstances (10%)
- Activities (40%)

It is argued that genes determine 50% of the happiness we feel throughout life.[6,11] Some scholars state that there is no sense in trying to be happier as genetics determine an individual's happiness "set point."[12] In other words, there are people who are just "naturally" happier than others.

---

[4] Researchers may define happiness in terms of positive/negative affect, optimism, life satisfaction, and pleasure vs. pain.

[5] The happiness model proposed by Lyubomirsky, Sheldon, & Schkade has been widely accepted in the happiness literature. The model is based on previous research studying heritability/genes and demographic/contextual influences on happiness.

[6] By genes I am referring to personality traits. Extraversion and neuroticism are most often connected to happiness. Scholars debate whether it is the personality trait that determines happiness or the fact that personality traits predispose a person to seek out activities. For example, a person who is extraverted will tend to seek out activities and experiences. Scholars argue that it is the activity and not the trait that determine happiness. McCrae, R. & Costa, P. (1991). Adding liebe und arbeit: The full five factor model and well-being. *Personality and Social Psychology Bulletin* 17, pp. 227–232.

Context (age, events, income, social class, education, location, etc.) is reported to have a smaller influence on happiness.[13] For example, research studies indicate that money (after a certain point) does not make you any happier. They argue that any increase in income after 90,000/year does not make anyone any happier.[14,15]

Scholars explain that many events that we experience, good or bad, are rapidly forgotten. Brickman, Coates, & Janoff-Bulman coined the term, "hedonic treadmill," which refers to the idea that people adapt to life events (e.g. winning the lottery, marriage, divorce, death of a loved one).[16] The effects events have on a person are transient.[7] Meaning that people's level of happiness does not change regardless of what happens to them.[8] After the event occurs, people adapt and become as happy or as miserable as they were before the event occurred.[9]

Researchers studied people who won the lottery and found that most went back to their "natural" happiness level after a period of time.[17] In the same manner, another researcher found that quadriplegics and paraplegics adapted to their circumstances after 2 months.[18] Researchers have continuously come across the fact that people are resilient and will maintain their level of well-being regardless of what happens to them.[19,20,21]

Although genetics and context are difficult things to control, we do have some control over the activities in

---

[7] People adapt to most events in less than three months. Suh, E., Diener, E., & Fujita, F. (1996). Events and subjective well-being: Only recent events matter. *Journal of Personality and Social Psychology, 70,* 1091-1102.

[8] Loewenstein & Frederick report that people adapt rapidly to some conditions, such as winning the lottery but slowly to others, such as the death of a beloved. Furthermore, people do not adapt, quickly or slowly, to some things such as the pleasure you get from food or sex. Loewenstein, G. & Frederick, S. (1997). Predicting Reactions to Environmental Change. In M. Bazerman, D. Messick, A. Tenbrunsel & K. Wade-Benzoni (Eds.), *Environment, Ethics, and Behavior.* San Francisco: New Lexington Press.

which we engage. Scholars state that forty percent of our happiness is determined by our engagement in pleasurable activities.[22] In other words, we can manipulate happiness by managing pleasurable activities. Furthermore, researchers argue that genetic and contextual influences can be overridden if activities are given more attention.[23] That is, your brain can be "rewired."[24] Hence, if you are born with particular genetic predispositions for happiness, your upbringing and context can change these genetic factors.

Furthermore, scholars argue that genes merely predispose you to engage in particular activities and that it is the activities in which you engage that influence your happiness.[25] In other words, having inherited a cheerful disposition will drive you to engage in social activities that will in turn provide you with happiness. However, if you do not have a cheerful disposition but engage in social activities, the engagement in social activities will make you happier, which will in turn will give you a more cheerful disposition. In the end, we may be lucky to get the happy gene or doomed if we don't, but engaging in particular behaviors can alter our luck.[26]

Researchers have found that happy people can list more enjoyable or pleasurable activities than those who are less happy. They state that happy people usually spend far more time, on average, doing such "fun" things.[27] In other words, happy people spend more time engaging in pleasure than others.[28]

A study at the University of Missouri compared students who made intentional changes in their activities (e.g. joining a club) to students who experienced a positive event (e.g. winning a scholarship) and found that the students who changed their activities had more sustained happiness than those who experienced a significant positive event in their lives.[29,30] Dr. Fordyce[10] found that accounts of well-being increased when he instructed his students to do what happy people do.[31] Dr. Fordyce has come up with 14 fundamental directives for happiness.[11] After detailed instruction on how to attain these directives, participants in his study showed increased well-being.

It doesn't take a bunch of research to see the logic behind the notion that adding more pleasure to our lives would make most of us happier. But the reality is we don't listen to this logic. We refrain from giving pleasure the importance that it deserves. A large number of us spend most of our time engaging in activities that are not pleasurable. Why do we go for a whole week or day without pleasure?

Some of us may answer that we don't have the time, money, and/or energy.[12] Or, that we have to make sure to work really hard in order to have fun in the future. Or even worse, we may say that we are not having fun regularly because it has become a habit.

I believe that many of these excuses are propelled by societal beliefs. People believe that pleasure will lead to social maladies such as unintended pregnancy, crime,

---

[10] Dr. Michael Fordyce is a major contributor to happiness theory and research. He has stated that most pleasurable activities identified by his research participants are low in cost and time.

[11] (a) keep busy and be more active; (b) spend more time socializing; (c) be productive at meaningful work; (d) get better organized and plan things out; (e) stop worrying; (f) lower your expectations and aspirations; (g) develop positive, optimistic thinking; (h) become present oriented; (i) work on a healthy personality; (j) develop an outgoing, social personality; (k) be yourself; (l) eliminate negative feelings and problems; (m) close relationships are the number one source of happiness; (n) put happiness as your most important priority. Cited from Fordyce, M. W. (1983). A program to increase happiness: Further studies. *Journal of Counseling Psychology*, 30, 4, 483-498.

addiction, etc. Furthermore, we adhere to societal beliefs that engagement in pleasure leads people away from hard work and progress — the basis of our economic system. Lastly, how hard a person works has become a manner by which many societies judge human value.

Hedonia vs. Eudaimonia

Scholars state that happiness can be achieved by way of hedonia or eudaimonia.[32,33] Hedonism refers to the experience of pleasure and eudaimonism refers to the experience of meaning making and self-development.[13,14,15,34] In general researchers give more importance to eudaimonia than hedonia.[35] They state that those who engage in hedonism experience momentary or fleeting experiences of happiness and those who engage in eudaimonia will have long lasting happiness.

Most of us would agree that long-term, meaningful, and growth inducing activities are better than momentary and "thoughtless" experiences of pleasure. However, when I went over the literature on happiness something didn't sit right for me. I knew my experience has been that of belonging to a group of people that constructs engaging in pleasure for the sake of pleasure

---

[13] The "daimon" in eudaimonism stands for your ideal sense of self, the truest and most congruent self you can be. In accordance, eudaimonism refers to activities that lead you to your daimon.

[14] Since before the birth of Christ, philosophers have been debating whether happiness is linked to eudaimonia (self-development) or to hedonia (momentary pleasure). Most of the time they take rather dichotomous stances on this topic. Aristippus of Cyrene stated that the only goal in life should be experiencing pleasure no matter the costs (hedonia). Aristotle, on the other hand, stated that engaging in pleasure is vulgar and that the goal in life should be virtue (eudaimonia). Still, Epicurus advocated for the belief that happiness should be about abstinence from bodily desires (eudaimonia).

as (inherently) meaningful. The scholarly discussions were different from my personal experiences. I concluded that the problem I perceived in the literature was rooted in the fact that the assumptions made by these scholars were not reflective of my lived experience.

The distinction between hedonia and eudaimonia may be unnecessary because it is based on the assumption that momentary or fleeting feelings of pleasure are not meaningful or growth producing in of themselves. In other words, scholars assume that eating a piece of chocolate, for example, does not contribute to long-term happiness because it is not growth producing or meaningful. I argue that it is meaningful, as long as experiencing pleasure is constructed as meaningful.[16]

In fact, research has found that people in happier nations give leisure time upmost importance. Furthermore, because valuing leisure time did not indicate less concern for the meaning of life in their studies, scholars conclude that hedonism "does not imply a superficial approach to life."[36]

Furthermore, engaging in pleasure has been documented to be instrumental to our emotional, cognitive and physical well-being.[37,38] When something is instrumental to our well-being, logic tells us that its pursuit is meaningful as well. It is simply a matter of thinking about pleasure in a different way.

---

[16] Veenhoven cites research studies that have not found a correlation between life goals of hedonism and increased life satisfaction. Although this is the information available right now, I feel the topic needs to be investigated further (as Veenhoven states as well). In the same publication, Veenhoven goes on to cite a global study (ARISE, 1986) indicating that the happiest nations reported more enjoyment and no guilt when engaging in hedonistic activities. This leads me to question whether the lack of guilt was based on values in regards to life and pleasure. Meaning that lack of guilt may be indicative of a positive value given to pleasure.

In the end, meaning is a social construction that is dependent on a social group and its context. Hence, researchers cannot distinguish with any exactitude whether it is the activity or the meaning given to the activity that produces long-term happiness. That is, meaning is not inherent to an activity but rather depends on social construction.

What Can Pleasure Do For You?

My assumption in writing this book is that increases in happiness and increases in pleasure go hand in hand. In other words, an increase in pleasurable activities will result in an increase in happiness. Hence, I conclude that experiencing pleasure is a primal component of happiness. Consequently, I claim that the benefits derived from happiness are the same as those for pleasure. My review of the happiness literature revealed the following benefits to being happy:[17]

Physical

- Energy and desire to be active[39,40]
- Strong immune system[41]
- Better health[42,43]
- Longer life[44,45]
- Physical arousal and excitement[46]
- Feelings of aliveness, vitality, and energy[47]
- Increased endorphins[48,49]
- Awareness of environment where senses come alive and the world becomes "richer and more vibrant"[50]

---

[17] The benefits listed would not be achieved from engaging in one pleasurable activity but rather from engaging in a life that values and pursues many different types of pleasures.

Cognitive

- Positive affect[51]
- Positive thinking[52]
- Pleasant memories and recollections[53]
- Good memory[54]
- Clearer thinking and focus[55,56]
- Fluency in thought processes[57]
- Decisive action[58]
- Present oriented[59]
- Development of the brain[60]
- Creativity[61,62,63]

Emotional

- Feeling that life is "full and abundant"[64]
- Feeling that life is more meaningful[65]
- Self control and mastery[66,67]
- Feelings of satisfaction, fulfillment, completion[68,69]
- Feelings of success and competency[70,71,72]
- Feeling closer to others and environment[73]
- Feelings of being loved and admired[74]
- Self-esteem and self-regard[75,76,77]
- Good mental health[78]
- Attainment of self ideal[79]
- Psychological resistance and resilience[80]
- Less likely to have substance abuse history[81]

Social

- Positive attitude towards others[82]
- Many friends[83,84]
- Rich social interactions[85]
- Self-confidence[86,87]
- Involvement in activities[88]
- Liked by others[89]

Global

- Pro-social and charitable behavior[90,91]
- Sense of freedom[92,93]
- Regard and respect for the world[94,95]
- Increased participation with environment[96,97]

Work

- Time at work goes much faster[98,99]
- Enjoyment satisfaction in work[100]
- Collaboration at work[101]
- Promotions/better evaluations[102]
- Ability to hired and get better jobs[103]
- More likely to graduate[104]

CHAPTER TWO

What is Pleasure?

Pleasure is the object, duty and the goal of all rational creatures. Voltaire

People react in two ways when I talk about pleasure. The first is by thinking that I am being kinky. The second is by becoming fearful that I will lead them onto the devil's path. Pleasure is immediately connected to excessive use of drugs and sex. It is equated with rampant abandonment of self and others.

Throughout history many people, religions, and schools of thought have believed that virtue, honesty, fellowship and health are compromised when we engage in pleasure. Pleasure has been blamed for a number of social problems including bankruptcy, corruption, poverty, drug addiction, rape, and suicide. Most people believe pleasure can be detrimental to long-term happiness.[105]

The United States has become a powerful nation because it has been dedicated to acts that are far removed from pleasure, such as hard work, diligence, austerity, and sacrifice. Our economic structures thrive on work ethics that promote disengagement from pleasure. It appears that many people are convinced that pleasure is dangerous. Researchers, on the other hand, are convinced that pleasure is necessary for a healthy and happy life and that we get physically and mentally ill without it.

The definitions provided by Webster's dictionary for pleasure are, "a state of being pleased," "sensual gratification," or "a source of delight or joy." Pleasure can occur before an act (anticipated pleasure), in the act, or after the act (remembered pleasure).[106] Pleasures are most often part of a process (before, during, and after) involving interaction with an object, thought, another living being, and/or feeling.

We often feel pleasure through physical sensations (touch, smell, sight, hearing), but we also feel pleasure through non-physical sensations (accomplishing a goal, fantasizing, understanding something, or experiencing art). Although pleasure is often divided into physical and non-physical pleasures, all pleasures involve a combination of physical and non-physical experiences. Our physical sensations influence our non-physical experiences and vice versa.

For example, when we feel pleasure after accomplishing a goal, it triggers chemical reactions (e.g.

dopamine) in the body that incite the reward centers in our brain. At the same time, when we feel pleasure from someone's touch, our thoughts and emotions are activated. All in all, physical and non-physical pleasures exist simultaneously as the body is always connected to the mind.

Pleasure Gloss

Scholars write that feeling pleasure involves accepting an experience and wanting more of it.[107,18] They argue that our brains place a "gloss" on experiences in order to decide how pleasurable they are or will be. Basically, the gloss is the value that we give an experience. So, if I smell bread, my brain places a gloss on the experience of smelling the bread. It places a value on the smell of bread. The value we give to an experience is determined by many factors.

Some scholars argue that value is determined by the usefulness of the experience. Hence, in the case of smelling bread, pleasure would be determined by how useful smelling bread is to us. Other scholars would say value is determined by whether or not an activity decreases pain. Consequently, the value of smelling bread would be determined by how much pleasure compared to pain we get when smelling bread. Still, other scholars contend that value is a function of whether or not the experience contributes to our survival. So, if smelling bread is necessary for our survival, we would derive more pleasure from it than if it was not. All in all, whether or not an experience is

---

[18] However, after a period of time, that the pleasure we derive diminishes. For example, when we are offered an ice cream, we decide we would like to engage in that pleasure for maybe one or two ice creams, but after a certain amount we become flooded and our pleasure diminishes.

pleasurable is partly dependent on the value we give to that experience.

The meanings we attach to experiences determine the value of that experience, and hence determine pleasure. Meaning making is a cognitive and emotional process influenced by social beliefs, customs, and attitudes. In other words, the meaning we give to an experience comes from our interactions with our social environment. Meanings can change dramatically with time and place.

For example, at this point in time in the United States, having intimacy with your partner means that the relationship is successful. However, intimacy would not be an indicator of a successful relationship in another country (Dominican Republic) or at another point in time (Victorian Age). To give another example, when my partner strokes me, I attach meaning to the stroking. I may understand that the stroking is a sign of love, given current American societal indoctrinations. Hence, the stroking *and* the thought that my partner loves me give me pleasure. Similarly, a meaning of love will provide me with more pleasure than a meaning of abuse.

Pleasure Rewards

The value we give an experience is generally determined by the rewards we gain in the following domains:

1. Sensory (heart beat change, muscle relaxation)
2. Social (monetary, power, relationships, identity)
3. Cognitive (sense of accomplishment, sense of identity, morality)
4. Emotional (love, joy, desire, relaxation, escape)

It is impossible that any one of these domains, in isolation from the others, results in pleasure. Social, cognitive, emotional, and sensory experiences are interdependent. They influence one another. For example, we cannot talk about sensory experiences without talking about cognitive experiences and vice versa. Hence, value is most often determined by how rewarding an experience is in more than one, if not all, of these domains. Think of a kiss – the pleasure experienced depends on the rewards received from the following:

(a) Sensory experience (feeling the softness and heat of another set of lips, heart racing, sexual urges)
(b) Social experience (potential for power, identity, etc.)
(c) Cognitive experience (the meaning we give to the kiss)
(d) Emotional experience (potential for love, resistance, relaxation).

To give another example, the pleasure experienced when looking at a piece of art will depend on the rewards received from the following:[108]

(a) Sensory experience (getting goose bumps or our heart may start racing)
(b) Social experience (we may feel connected to others or to the artist)
(c) Cognitive experience (we may think about the time and skill that was necessary to produce the work of art or about color, line, and composition)
(d) Emotional experience (the piece or art may bring out feelings of sadness, hope, fear).

An increase in any one domain will most likely lead to an increase in another domain because of their interdependence. Hence, if I increase the pleasures that are cognitively based, the pleasures I experience in the other domains will also increase. To give an example, exercise makes my body feel good in a physical/sensory manner. Consequently, feeling good physically makes me think about the world in a different manner. Thinking and feeling good makes me feel more confident and more able to connect with others. In the end, feeling pleasure involves social, emotional, cognitive, and sensory experiences in one way or another.

The Variety in Pleasure

Pleasure varies from individual to individual even when they reside in the same social environment. Pleasure will vary in intensity from person to person because we are all attracted to different pleasures.[109] What is pleasurable for one person may not be for another. In a similar vein, the pleasure one individual derives from an experience (e.g., sex) changes throughout life depending on age, surroundings, health, etc. The extent of the pleasure we feel depends on our external state and internal states.

External states include quality, expectation, and frequency. For example, I will feel more pleasure from eating steak than from eating ground beef (quality). I also will feel more pleasure if the meat is served by the best chef in the world (expectation and quality). Quantity also determines pleasure. The pleasure derived from eating ice cream changes depending how many ice creams have been eaten already and whether one more ice cream is useful to us.

Internal states include genetic endowment, health, emotional and cognitive abilities, and physical states. Genes may draw one to some pleasures and not others. Similarly, emotional and cognitive abilities will determine the extent or quality of pleasure one feels. Additionally, the state of health that an individual possesses will determine how able they are to experience pleasure. Lastly, physical states, such as when one is hungry, hot, or horny will determine the extent of pleasure they feel.

Irrational Pleasures

Although I discuss the experience of pleasure as something logical, calculated, and conscious, it really is not. Rarely do we sit down and make a list of rewards in each area of life when deciding how much pleasure we are feeling. Most often experiencing pleasure happens instantaneously and with an unnoticeable thought process. There are times when experiencing pleasure does not even happen in a conscious state.[110] Researchers have noted that the brain registers pleasure responses to events that are experienced unconsciously.[111] Similarly, many pleasurable experiences occur outside of our awareness.[112] For example, I may take a shower everyday but not equate it to pleasure because,

- I am not giving it attention
- It has become a habit
- I am not used to saying that things feel good
- Taking a shower has never been presented to me as something that can be relished and enjoyed
- I am not in touch with sensations in my body

The Language of Pleasure

The language we use determines pleasure. Pleasure is not a word in some languages, but in every language there are words that connote feeling good.[113] Language is important because it determines thoughts, feelings, and awareness. Although we can express pleasure without verbal language (through a smile), language holds possibilities for constraint and expansion of feelings, thoughts, and awareness.

To give an example, if I become sexually attracted to someone, I feel something different in my body and there is no need for language. But if I attach language, such as "sexual desire," to the experience, then the feeling is open to transformation. If the words "sexual desire" have a bad connotation, the sexual attraction that I feel in my body is transformed. At the same time, if "sexual desire" has a positive meaning, the feeling is transformed as well. Additionally, many people connect the word "pleasure" to evil and have a hard time labeling their experiences as pleasurable. In the end, the meaning behind the word "pleasure" transforms the bodily experience of pleasure as well.

The Importance of Pleasure

Scholars have noted that a lack of pleasure in life leads to particular undesirable emotional and mental states.[114] Depression, schizophrenia, addiction, anxiety, and obesity have been reported to be indicative of a "missing ability to experience pleasure."[115] Pleasure appears to be necessary for a healthy emotional life.

Pleasure helps us get in touch with ourselves as it forces us to identify our needs, wants, and desires. In order to engage in activities that are pleasurable, we must know what we enjoy. It is a common belief in the psychotherapy world that a strong sense of self is healthy. We may find that after some dedication to making pleasure important, we become less ruled by what others want and think and more loyal to our own needs, desires and thoughts. This is often the goal of psychotherapy and a successful approach to healing emotionally.

In the documentary by National Geographic, *Stress: Portrait of a Killer*, it is reported that chronic stress is fatal. The researchers found that the animals in their research studies with low levels of dopamine (pleasure) have the most stress. They go on to state that stress is responsible for numerous ailments in U.S. society including obesity, diabetes, heart problems, etc. They argue that Americans are in awe of people who are superhuman in terms of managing work and responsibilities. Americans value those who are stressed out rather than valuing a more balanced and stress free life.

The Pleasure in Pain

All in all, our goal in life is to be happier, not more miserable. Sometimes achieving this goal is not so simple. There are moments where displeasure and pain are more functional than pleasure. For example, sadness and depression may very well be more functional than happiness and pleasure would be for someone who needs to rest from stress would be. Furthermore, the most profound growth experiences many times come from pain, not pleasure. Pain can be as important to well-being as pleasure. Problems result when pain overtakes other feelings and when we feel pleasure less than pain.

Personally, I would rather entertain pain once or twice a week and pleasure three times per day. Would that make me less able to grow? I don't think so because I can grow rather rapidly from my painful experiences and then move on to engage in more pleasant activities. In the end, unhappiness exists when pain stays for as long as it desires, stalking and tormenting us.

Addiction and Pleasure

The question I am most frequently asked when I discuss pleasure is, "What about addiction and pleasure?" Addiction and pleasure are often believed to go hand in hand. One engages with drugs because it is immensely pleasurable. The alcoholic drinks to find pleasure; the sex addict fucks for pleasure.

However, the pleasure that an alcoholic or heroin addict feels is different from the pleasure for which I advocate. The pleasure that is part of an addiction takes one away from oneself and one's surroundings. The addict engages in pleasure in order to escape from pain and from reality. The type of pleasure that is connected to happiness, on the other hand, is one that gets a person more in tune with their bodies, surroundings, and feelings, and not one that is an escape from the same.

Pleasure In a Nutshell

To summarize, the pleasure we feel from an experience (e.g., eating steak) is dependent on the following:[116]

1. Value (Is eating steak valuable to my life in terms of survival or usefulness?)
2. Meaning (Does eating steak mean something good?)
3. Language (Do we attach the word "pleasure" to eating steak and do we define "pleasure" as good?)
4. External state (What is the quality of steak, the cook, and quantity of the steak?).[19]
5. Internal state (Are we hungry or full? Are we sick?)
6. Beliefs and expectations (Do we expect that the steak will be good?)

---

[19] This is not accurate if someone is used to eating ground beef and not steak.

CHAPTER THREE

Understanding Pleasure in Your Life

How have you spent the last year of your life? Have your days been filled with vigor, liveliness, glory and thrill? Have you wanted to jump out of bed with the excitement and anticipation for the glorious day ahead of you?

This chapter will help you determine how much pleasure you have in your life. It will also aid you in understanding your beliefs about pleasure and its connection to your lifestyle. Consequently, you will gain insight as to what you need to do in order to increase pleasure.

Pleasure Scale

This exercise will identify your current level of engagement in pleasure. Dr. Fordyce found that the happiest people list over 25 items but that the average is 10-15 items.[117]

List all the pleasurable activities in which you engage each day for a week. List these activities after each day is completed. After each activity note what your mood is like when and after doing these activities.

When I completed the pleasure scale I became acutely aware of my likes and dislikes. I learned that things that were pleasurable to me in the past where not as pleasurable any more and that I needed to change some aspects of my life to gain that experience of pleasure again. For instance, drinking coffee was not as pleasurable as I had known it to be. I tried to implement things to make it more pleasurable like going outside to drink it or buying coffee that was of higher quality.

Another thing I realized was that if I changed little things such as making sure I had something that I really liked for breakfast, or making my bed more comfortable, or making sure I didn't rush myself made me happier. The smallest details were very important to my experience of pleasure.

How Comfortable Are You with Pleasure?

In order to figure out how comfortable you are with the concept of pleasure, you need to understand how you have defined pleasure throughout your life. It is important to understand where you are coming from in order to identify where you want to go because your past could get in the way of change.

For example, when I said that I wanted to have more pleasure in my life I didn't think about my definition of pleasure. I didn't think about why I thought about pleasure the way that I did. Eventually, obstacles started to materialize. There was point where I felt doubtful that I had done the right thing by focusing on pleasure even though it felt really good. If I had known beforehand that these feelings would come up given my history with pleasure, it would have been easier to cope with.

In order to understand your ideas about pleasure and where they come from, take some time to be by yourself without distractions and answer the following questions:

1. How do your caretakers view and engage in pleasure?
2. How do other people in your family view and engage in pleasure?
3. How do your friends view and engage in pleasure?
4. How do you view and engage in pleasure?
5. Are there any similarities or differences in these answers?

My mother's side of the family follows work ethics of honor, diligence, and sacrifice. They amaze me in their ability to create and maintain wealth and security. Yet, when it comes to pleasure, they are not so dedicated. For example, my mother has always helped me by taking care of my children if I needed to work but she would never take care of them if I wanted to go out with friends or indulge in any other pleasurable activity. The belief that we should not engage in pleasure is so extreme in my family that I found myself hiding from her, as an adult, when I was doing anything that was not work related. I tell you this story because you may have similar ones. There were many times I felt guilty and silly. It's ironic, or not, that in the end I was able to engage openly in pleasure in front of my mother because I was writing a book and composing videos about it. Some things never change!

These exercises are designed to help you learn about your own definition of pleasure and how others influence those definitions. As you move through this process, be aware that friends and family around you may resist or even oppose what you are doing–stay strong!

Does Displeasure Work for You?

The definition of displeasure is "feeling unhappy, uncomfortable, and disappointed." Feeling displeasure works in some way for all of us, meaning that in some way it helps to feel displeasure. It is difficult to understand how something painful can actually be functional.

When I started thinking about pleasure I realized that not having pleasure in my life was necessary in order for me to maintain an obsessive and addictive relationship to many things in my life. I found that when I got excited about something such as a new project or a new relationship that I couldn't concentrate on anything else; I was elated and manic. I worked on it constantly and with great energy. Eventually, however, I couldn't maintain that level of a high, so I crashed (displeasure). Afterwards, I felt disillusioned, tired, and beaten up. The feeling of displeasure when I crashed was functional because it allowed me to refuel my energy for forthcoming excitement.

In the end, the process of extreme highs and lows were debilitating for me because they promoted the exclusion of things that were not part of my obsession at that moment. I learned that hyper focusing on anything led me to exclude time with friends and family, for example.

Consequently, I've realized that if I make changes in my behavior where I am constantly being pleasured, I don't have the need for extreme highs and lows. In other words, if I purposefully and routinely incorporate things that pleasure me, it decreases my need for extreme highs and lows. The explanation I give is that the involvement in the extreme high (pleasure) is probably indicative of a lack of pleasure in my life.

In order to find out how displeasure works for *you* in your life, let's do the following exercise. Write down all the feelings you have throughout the day on an hourly basis. Do this for two days. After you are done ask yourself the following questions:

1. What kept you from feeling good?
2. What would have happened at that moment if you changed your mood to a good one? What would be the consequences?
3. Why did you feel good in the moments you felt good?
4. Overall, did you observe any patterns involved in feeling good and/or feeling bad?

The idea behind this exercise is to understand why it is that displeasure and pleasure make their appearance at certain times during the day and at certain times during your life. It's important to understand that it is not about labeling events as good or bad. Rather, that we be aware of our conscious and proactive choices to experience pleasure and displeasure in our lives.

Your Definition of Pleasure

If you feel prepared to write down a definition of pleasure, take the time to do it now. For those of you who are unsure about how to do this, use the following prompts to guide you:

1. Feeling pleasure has been a way for me to....
2. Engaging in pleasure has made me feel...
3. Engaging in pleasure has made me think...
4. Feeling pleasure allows me to...
5. Feeling pleasure means that I...
6. When I engage in pleasure I feel...
7. Not engaging in pleasure means...
8. When I engage in pleasure I think...
9. When I engage in pleasure others feel...
10. When I engage in pleasure other think...
11. Society says pleasure is...
12. My family says pleasure is...
13. Pleasure is something that...

My definition of pleasure when I started went something like this:

Feeling pleasure is a way for me to forget about my reality. It's a way to escape from my family's strict guidelines about what I should be doing. It's a way to express myself intensely. Engaging in pleasure makes me feel alive. Engaging in pleasure means that I am being irresponsible. Feeling pleasure allows me to do things that I usually cannot do.

Feeling pleasure means that I will be punished and that will have to pay for engaging in it. Not engaging in pleasure means that I am old and boring. When I engage in pleasure I think I am getting away with something. When I engage in pleasure others feel scared and angry. When I engage in pleasure others think that I am being irresponsible. Society says that pleasure is dangerous.

My definition shows the struggle I had with pleasure. It shows that I felt that I needed to choose between doing the "right thing" and pleasuring myself. I didn't feel that pleasure was something I should be doing. I struggled with wanting to experience pleasure but feeling like I shouldn't because of my definition of it as bad. I gave into pleasure in an uncontrollable way rather than in a purposeful way.

A New Definition of Pleasure

Take your definition of pleasure and rewrite it in a way that reflects how you would like pleasure to function in your life from this day forward. My new definition of pleasure is the following:

Feeling pleasure is a way for me to gain perspective on my reality. It's a way that will help me manage my multiple familial obligations. It's a way to express myself intensely. Expressing myself is necessary and healthy. Engaging in pleasure makes me feel alive. Engaging in pleasure means that I am being responsible because I am taking care of myself and attending to my needs. Feeling pleasure helps me experiment with different things and this is healthy because it provides me with perspective and solutions. Feeling pleasure means that I will be rewarded with more functionality in life. Not engaging in pleasure means that I am not taking care of myself. When I engage in pleasure I think I am doing what I should be doing in order to lead a happy and healthy life. When I engage in pleasure others feel scared and angry, and that will be something they will have to handle. I cannot control the feelings and thoughts of others. When I engage in pleasure others think that I am being irresponsible, and this, again, is their problem. I know I am being more responsible to myself by engaging in pleasure. Society says that pleasure is dangerous. I've decided I'm not contributing to social control. Everyone differs in his or her definition of pleasure. This definition is mine for me to live by.

I've obviously changed my perception of pleasure. I now understand that pleasure is necessary in my life and that I need to be intentional about incorporating it. I need to make it a priority because it will make me happy and keep me in touch with what makes me feel good. I've found that if I am continually feeding my needs to feel good then I am creating a more solid sense of self and therefore teaching others and myself that I am important. No longer is my pleasure about being cool or about losing control but about really loving myself.

Do You Need a Reason to Engage in Pleasure?

Yes! At this point in time, you need a reason to engage in pleasure because you may encounter resistance. You need it so that you can repeat it to yourself and others in times of difficulty. What will be your reason for engaging in pleasure? Use your new definition of pleasure to come up with a couple of sentences that will state your reasons. Mine is the following:

I have a right to do what feels good to my body. I want to be as happy as I can be. Being happy is good for everyone. Pleasuring myself is something that is good for me emotionally, physically, and spiritually.

Now that we have a definition for pleasure in our lives and we have a reason to pleasure ourselves, lets find out exactly how to incorporate more pleasure into our lives.

CHAPTER FOUR

Creating Your Hedonic Palate

After you complete the exercises in this chapter you should have a master list of pleasurable activities. It is important to have a list of things that give you pleasure because it will provide you with an indication of what you need to increase or decrease in your life so that you maximize your happiness.

Additionally, it is important to have a list of pleasures in order to go on to the next section of this book, *Expanding Your Hedonic Palate*. Researchers have noted that happy people engage in a variety of pleasurable activities and that their attitude is one of exploration and innovation in life. Hence, in order to maximize happiness, we should nurture what we already find pleasurable (your current list) while exploring different experiences (your expanded list).

Ideal Life

Imagine that you have no limits and that you are doing anything you want. Don't think of time, money, family, or health. What would your life look like? Think of the different areas in your life such as financial, relational, emotional, physical, and spiritual. Take a few minutes and write down this vision. You can use the following prompts to guide you:

1. What would you be doing on a day-to-day basis? Where and what time would you wake up? Where would you be? Who would be with you? How would you wake up? Why would you wake up? What would you do next?
2. What would you be working at? Who would be working with you? How would you be working? Why would you be working?
3. How much money would you have? How would you receive this money? Why would you be getting this money?
4. What would be your most important relationships? How would you be involved? What would the relationships look like? Why would you be in these relationships?
5. Where would you live? Who would you live with? How would you live? What would surroundings look like? Why would you live here?
6. What would your body be like? How would you take care of it? Why would you have the body you have?

Now look for clues about what gives you pleasure in your description of the ideal life. For me it was travel, hanging out, physical surroundings, food, shopping, my children, eating with my children, writing, making videos, controversy, thought, cooking, entertaining, road trips, new experiences, spontaneity, going out, partying, dancing, expression of self, having a maid, exercise, and movies. Make sure you write down pleasures in the positive way. In other words, don't write down that a pleasure is "not doing housework" but rather name it, "having a maid."

Pleasure Memories

Go back to your first memory and start writing down your happiest moments from this point on. Sit down quietly and alone for at least an hour while doing this. Try to stay with each memory for a few minutes remembering all the details. Write down whatever it is no matter how silly it is. Don't filter anything. Whatever comes into your head write it down, even if you know that those types of things don't make you happy right now.

After you are done pulling up a memory or a time in your life, ask yourself what exactly made you happy about that moment. Think about your senses (touch, feel, hearing, sight and smell) when answering this question. What were you were seeing, smelling, feeling, touching that made you happy? What were your thoughts at this moment? You can also ask your family members whether they remember things that you liked to do when you where younger. Once you are done identifying the specifics of the moments that made you happy, add them to you list.

Sensory Pleasures

Think about the most talked about senses (sight, hearing, taste, touch, and smell) and list the things that have been pleasurable for you. For the sense of smell, for example, my pleasures are pine, rosemary, fire, food, roasts, my grandmother's closet, flowers, perfumes, my children's scent, incense, snow, rain, beach, new cars, clean sheets, hung dry clothes, soaps, and cedar. Some of these smells can be decomposed in order to provide more precision. For example, my desire for soaps could be decomposed to denote which types of soaps I have preference for. Which soaps are more pleasurable than others? Take some time to complete this exercise for each one of your senses and add the items to your list. Remember not to filter anything. Write anything that comes up no matter how ridiculous it may seem.

Favorite Times and People

Think of your favorite times during the day, month and year and add these to your list. Then write down the specific things that you enjoyed about that day, month, or year. When I identified October as my favorite time during the year, I identified the following specific pleasures: the chill, the color of the sky, the smell in the air, the falling leaves, and my birthday. I added these items to my list but I also left October as a pleasure in itself. Of course you can't make October come more than once a year, but you can psyche yourself up (much like major holidays) for this time.

Take some time to think of your favorite people. Think about the specific things that give you pleasure about these people and add them to your list. Also, add those people to your list so that you remember to nurture these important relationships.

Free Pleasure

Spend two days doing whatever you want without any limitations. Try to keep your responsibilities to a minimum and only do them if you want. The idea behind this exercise is to identify your intrinsic motivations. Knowing what motivates you intrinsically will help you identify what motivates you without any external influence. So, if you want to dance all morning long, you do it because it is something that you would do no matter the reward or no matter what is happening externally at that moment.

Unfortunately, or not, I found that even when I could do whatever I wanted for a whole day, I wanted to sit down in front of the computer and write. I knew that in my life I would write regardless of whether I was paid for it or whether someone thought my writing was good or not. In other words, I am intrinsically motivated to write.

When I did this exercise I found myself relishing every moment of those two days. When I ate, I didn't think of shoving something in my mouth but rather about what would give me pleasure. So I ate less and only what was really pleasurable. Everything happened in slow motion those days. Even the menial tasks such as washing the dishes became pleasurable. I think this happened because attending to pleasure gives one the opportunity to connect to the moment and that moment becomes important. Every detail becomes noticeable and time slows down. Hence, no matter what the activity is, the act of focusing on details and slowing things down is pleasurable in itself.

Sometimes during those two days, I found myself wandering without an idea of what to do. I was laying in my bed feeling a bit anxious. There wasn't anything particular that I could do at that moment that would give me pleasure, but I lied very still and sat with the feeling of anxiety. I let it run through my body and made no attempt to rationalize it or do anything about it. I began to feel peaceful and in my stillness I became aware of the silence of the night. The more stillness I achieved, the more in awe I became of the darkness around me. My stillness and letting go allowed me to experience one of the most pleasurable moments in my life.

Moments where you don't know how to pleasure yourself are extremely difficult. I found that it is usually an indication that I need to relax and just sit with myself. If this doesn't work, I force myself to go through my list of pleasures and experience one after the other until I feel better. Sometimes our bodies and minds are accustomed to being miserable and we have to force them to be happy.

Deconstructing Your Pleasures

Identifying details in your experiences of pleasure is extremely important because it allows you to become precise about the things that pleasure you. As I noted previously, it allows you to build a stronger sense of self because it allows you to get to know what you desire and need.

Take some time now and look at each item on your list. Think about the reasons a particular item gave you pleasure or made you happy. Some things won't need deconstruction such as the smell of rosemary, but others will, such as your favorite people. What exactly is it about that person that gives you pleasure? What sight, smells, touches, and hearing are involved? If you say you like hanging out with your best friend, what is it exactly that you like about being with him/her? Does it involve touch, smell, hearing, sight, or some other thing?

Your Master List of Pleasures

You should have a rather extensive list of items that give you pleasure. Sort it out and take out duplicates. Finding duplicates will help you see how important some pleasures are in your life. The "beach" appeared four times for me, which means that I should incorporate the beach into my life on a regular basis. One thing that was a surprise for me was that the word "woods" came up six times. I didn't realize that being in the woods gave me so much pleasure.

Go through and highlight in green the pleasures that you engage in already. Next highlight in yellow those pleasures that you have at your disposal that you do not engage in on a regular basis. These are the pleasures that are important to start consciously and purposefully incorporating into your life because they probably don't require any extra effort or cost. Take some time to make a plan about how you will do this before moving on. For example, my list included enjoying the sunset. However, I haven't been able to enjoy it because I live in an apartment. I decided to change my running time to the late afternoon in order to enjoy the sunset. Tack your to do list on the wall or desktop so you don't forget to incorporate these pleasures immediately.

Identify the pleasures that are not accessible to you and place them on a wish list. Tack this list somewhere you will see everyday as well. Although these items may appear to be big and unattainable right now, you may be able to enjoy a smaller version of them. I'll give you an example. One of my greatest pleasures is sex, but right now I can't have sex. So, instead I can masturbate. Not the same, I know, but it is a mini version of the bigger pleasure.

Once you place the pleasure wish list in a place you can refer to everyday, you are 80% closer to fulfilling those wishes. I make it a habit to read my narrative about my ideal life and my pleasure wishes every morning when I get up. I also read over my list of pleasures that I have readily available to me so that I am reminded to keep incorporating them into my life. These lists and narratives keep me motivated and focused. They give me energy and strength to get through the times where my mind or people try to convince me to stop pleasuring myself.

There have been so many things that I have wanted but never got. Once I started to write down my wishes or goals and reread them on a regular basis, they materialized. When I first started this process, I was skeptical. I decided I would prove that this was a stupid idea and wrote down the most impossible wish. I wrote, "I want to get up every morning and have a leisurely breakfast. I want to write all morning and exercise in the afternoon." For a single mother working full time, I perceived this wish to be impossible. But, guess what I am doing now?

Pleasures I Am Engaging In

Intellectual Stimulation	Creativity	Beautiful people
Breeze	Challenges	Children
City Sounds	Clean sheets	Early mornings
Family Time	Getting New Ideas	Hung dry clothes
Essential Oils	Innovation	Laughing
Learning	Mondays	Movies
Music	My children's scent	Naps
Rain	Reading	Rosemary
Running	Sleeping	Sunlight
Writing	Sweat	Warm weather
Calling in Sick	Running in the Rain	Water
Singing	Lip Gloss	A Quiet Morning
Hanging Out	Expression of Self	Making Videos
Eating with my Family	Walking in the Rain	

Available Pleasures in which I Am Not Engaging

A Beautiful Home	Artwork	The Ocean
Cedar	Drawing	Walking Barefoot
Entertaining	Flowers	Food
Herbs	Making Things	Moon
Organization	Partying	Rustle of a Tree
Sunset	Small Spaces	Sunbathing
Driving with the Windows Down	Candles	Dancing

Pleasures Not Available to Me: My Wish List

Lighting/Color	Color	December
Fashion/Shopping	Country Side	A Lover's Scent
Fire	Roasts	New Cars
Crispy Weather	Sex	Perfume
Pine	Travel	Soaps
Wind Chimes	Skinny Dipping	Snow
BBQs	Road Trips	Woods

PART II

EXPANDING YOUR HEDONIC PALATE

In embracing diversity, we will find true happiness --
Malcolm Gladwell[118]

Once you have created a master list of pleasures it is important to expand on that list. It would be a shame to limit yourself to your particular experiences of pleasure. In order to grow, we need to push our limits. Engaging in pleasure requires that we challenge our comfort zones and exert ourselves to go a little bit further every time. It is similar to exercise where muscles get stronger every time you go beyond the customary limits.

The more we engage in pleasurable activities, the happier most of us will be. The shorter your list of pleasures, the unhappier you are, according to Dr. Fordyce. Happy people have long list of pleasures because they are open to new experiences.

Psychologists argue that the key to happiness is variety and innovation and that embracing discomfort and new ways of doing things are key vehicles to self-development and growth. Innovation has been argued to be an important component of happy people's life style. Researchers have noted that happy people devote themselves to trying new things and to having many different types of pleasures in their life.

New experiences have been shown to get dopamine levels flowing in the body. Dopamine is the feel good chemical. Researchers say that novel experiences push you to decide to act and the decision to act increases the levels of dopamine in your body.[119] Hence, the more willing you are to experiment with new things, the happier you will be. If you find pleasure in eating chocolate cake, go a step further and try some chocolate covered strawberries, for example.

Novelty doesn't have to be something extraordinary such as jumping of a cliff or eating frog legs. It could be as simple as eating a lollipop you haven't eaten for a decade, taking a nap in the middle of the day, listening to a song you haven't heard in a while, or trying out a new genre of music.

The important point is to commit to taking opportunities that come to you on a daily basis. It's about having a curious attitude. For example, instead of having the attitude of "Yuk" when a co-worker offers you a taste of her sushi, you have the attitude of "Yes! I'll try anything once!" The thinking changes from being put off to being thankful and in awe of new opportunities.

Sometimes the opposite is true as well, and giving up old pleasures is as innovative as incorporating new pleasures. We maintain a sense of amazement and curiosity when we momentarily stop doing something pleasurable. For example, when I ate my first piece of bread after being on a diet, I felt that I was engaging in the most decadent pleasure. Have you noticed that sleeping in your bed for the first time after being away is so much more pleasurable than when you sleep in it day after day?

In the end, maximizing pleasurable experiences is about managing pleasure. One can stop and savor and then focus and heighten, for example. You can manage pleasure the same way you can manage an orgasm. For some, orgasms are better when one "plays" with them and extends or prolongs the moment of buildup to climax.

Think about what you can do differently today. Can you eat or wear something different? Try out small things so that it doesn't cause fatigue or involve a lot of physical effort. You don't have to go out shopping for new clothes or get on a plane to India. Begin with what you have. I made the mistake of wanting to do drastic things, such as moving to a different country. What I should have done was to focus on average moments. So instead of going out to the supermarket to find exciting and new food you can find something that is easy to change and that involves what you immediately have available.

For example, if you watch television every night, challenge yourself to not watch it for a week. Or if you rush in the morning, try taking your time for a few days, even if it means being late. Something as small as a new bar of soap will excite those senses into pleasure!

Having highlighted the importance of innovation, it is important to state that although innovation has been shown to increase happiness, the old or customary are also important. We are pleasured by new and exciting things such as going to a new country or by listening to new music, but we are also pleasured by what has been around for a while such as an old blanket, old pictures, a song from the past, etc. The key is to identify the old things that give you pleasure while you open your mind and heart to experiencing new pleasures.

Finally, some pleasures, in my opinion, should not be messed with because the high is so intense. Things such as sex and exercise come to my mind. I don't think we need to stop doing these things in order to get more pleasure out of them. Alternatively, I suggest varying the way that we do them. Instead of running every day, for example, I have incorporated other types of exercises as well. Personal trainers advocate that the best thing for your body is to vary the types of exercises that you do. The same goes for pleasure.

In the following chapters I have assembled a list of pleasurable activities by compiling and categorizing the information I found in research articles, Internet searches, informal conversations with people, and personal experiences.[120,121,122,123] It was difficult to separate activities into categories as most activities have elements of more than one category. I simply chose the most salient category for each item.

The following chapters will help you expand your list of pleasurable activities. My discussions on each category will explain the reasons that these activities are pleasurable so that you can be creative and identify activities not listed. Additionally, you will have the information you need to backup your pleasure-seeking activities in moments of resistance. For example, hanging out with friends is listed as pleasurable because it provides for social contact. If you know that most people find social connection to be pleasurable because they get validation, then you can come up with your own social activities, such as spending time with pets. Also, when someone states that you care too much about hanging out with friends, for example, you can state that research shows that social connection is an integral part of happiness.

I have developed the following categories to classify pleasurable activities:

1. **Social Connection**
   a. Validation/Belonging
   b. Self-Grooming
   c. Intimacy and Love
   d. Giving Back
2. **Escape/Relaxation**
   a. Sleeping/Napping/Daydreaming
   b. Spirituality/Meditation
   c. Laughter/Humor
   d. Books/TV/Movies
3. **Physical/Sensory**
   a. Touch
   b. Rocking/Motion
   c. Sexuality
   d. Exercise/Sports
   e. Eating/Cooking
   f. Sensation Seeking
4. **Mastery**
   a. Creation
   b. Learning
   c. Completion
   d. Recognition
5. **Environment**
   a. Home/Domestic Life
   b. Nature
   c. Light/Color
   d. Aroma
   e. Sound/Music

CHAPTER FIVE

Social Connection

Kissing, flirting, telling someone how much you love them, teaching, volunteering, gift giving, counseling, getting your hair done, putting on make up, shopping, tanning, hanging out with friends, chatting, talking, email, weddings, births, graduations, criticizing others

Researchers and therapists often prescribe social contact and support when increasing well-being. Happy people engage in more social activities than those who are not as happy.[124] Scholars maintain that in order to have a happy and satisfying life, we must have connections with others. Furthermore, it has been noted that those of us with strong social networks and connections fare better in situations of adversity.

Many pleasurable experiences can be classified as social activities, such as hanging out or chatting with friends. However, researchers have noted that it's not merely the engagement in social activities that promotes well-being but rather a sense of being connected to a social group or person. The connection brings about feelings of validation, belonging, security, and trust. In turn, these feelings bring about pleasure.

Validation/Belonging

Humans need to feel that they belong somewhere.[125] Experiences that help us feel that we belong are frequently described as pleasurable experiences, such being popular or going to a family gathering. Even criticizing others is pleasurable because it provides a way to ensure a part in the group.

Validation is another important component to belonging. Experiences of validation such as being complimented, having someone agree with you, or getting a hug, are often noted to be pleasurable. Pleasure is also experienced when we validate others such as when we cheer someone on, compliment someone, or smile at someone.

When we feel we belong, we get a sense of security and self-identity. Comparing ourselves to those within and outside of a group, answers the question "Who am I?" Likewise, we find pleasure in watching and talking about others. We have fun "people watching" with friends. We determine who we are by watching and categorizing others. We like to hypothesize about others' intentions, values and lifestyle by observing what they do. "People watching," to give one example, fulfills our needs to be validated (e.g. Do I look as good as she does?). And when we feel we belong, we feel secure.

On the other hand, there are social connections that are not good for us. Researchers have highlighted that it is not the quantity of social connections that gives us pleasure, but rather the quality of these relationships.[126] It is our perception of whether a social connection is good or not that gives us pleasure, not the connection in itself. Hence, engagement in social activities does not ensure pleasure. Similarly, engaging in larger quantities of social activities does not equate with greater pleasure in life. However, social connections are crucial to our survival and a source of great pleasure to most of us. The key is to maximize the good connections and minimize the bad connections.

Self-Grooming

Researchers have argued that the way we feel about our appearance can have significant effects on our well-being.[127] Self-grooming may be pleasurable because of our need to connect to others. The better we look, the more we are liked and the more we fit in. Or, self-grooming may help us with our perception of self. The closer to an ideal sense of self we get, the better we feel about ourselves. For example, if my ideal self is to be thin, the closer I get to this ideal self, the happier I will be. Likewise, self-grooming helps us focus on our bodies and ourselves, making this attention to self pleasurable. It gives us a sense of self-realization and/or actualization.[128,129]

Lastly, self-grooming may be pleasurable because it helps us get things in life.[130] Research has shown that beautiful people get more things. They argue that attractive people experience better social and psychological outcomes than unattractive people.[131] They get a better mate, a better job, more promotions, more salaries, better treatment, better grades, and people tend to think more highly of them.[132]

It is difficult to say which comes first, beauty or happiness, and it really doesn't matter for the purposes of this discussion. We know that self-grooming activities are pleasurable and consequently should be given some importance.

Intimacy and Love

A source of great pleasure for most of us is intimacy and love. In his book, *Love and Survival*, Dr. Ornish, clinical professor of Medicine at the University of California, San Francisco presents research that documents how activities that promote intimacy and love are healing.[133] Not only that, but he argues that love and intimacy are protective factors against disease.

The reasons abound as to why we are so in love with love. One being that it increases chemicals such as dopamine (feel good chemical) and oxytocin (bonding hormone that makes us feel safe) in our bodies. Another reason being that romantic love ensures the survival of humans as it maximizes the chances that we propagate.

Finally, romantic activities make us feel special. Feeling that we belong to a group, as I discussed previously, is often balanced with needs of feeling special and different from the group. As we have a need to belong, we also have a need to be unique. Having someone love you makes you feel special and different from the rest. Having someone tell you that they can't live without you and that they have never met anyone like you provides you with feelings of specialness that give pleasure.

Non-romantic relationships are also a source of great pleasure in that they create the same feelings of being special, such as being a leader of a group, or being popular, or being/having a best friend. In both romantic and non-romantic relationships it is pleasurable to feel special. When we feel special we feed our need to belong, to trust and to be cared for.

Having stated this, I have to say that although I know and respect the importance of intimacy and love that this category has become somewhat enslaving. First, the pleasure we feel as a result of intimacy and love is often times tied to the meaning and importance we give to the same. An overwhelming number of our social narratives focus on how common and life-altering love and intimacy are. Most of us feel that unless we engage in these experiences, there is something wrong with us. Our perceptions of self depend on how close we get to social narratives regarding love and intimacy. We end up focusing most of our energies on love and intimacy, which leaves us with little energy and time to devote to other pleasurable activities.

Giving Back

As we find pleasure in receiving, be it love or money, we find pleasure in giving as well. The ability to give provides many people with pleasure. The world would not survive unless people gave back to each other and to society. We need people to share knowledge, money, food, time, love, etc. If not, parents would not take care of children, or the strong would not help the weak.

Giving provides us with the opportunity to ensure our individual survival. By giving to another, we assure our future in getting help when we need it. Many times parents raise their children in order to ensure that they will be taken care of when older or sick. Society is inundated with messages regarding karma and how important it is to give or be good so that nothing bad happens.

Giving gets us closer to social ideals of what it means to be a "good" citizen. If you are kind and help others, you are getting closer to idealized notions of a "good" person.

Regardless of the reasons for giving, many people experience it as pleasurable. Hence, find ways to give but make sure you are in a position to give. Sometimes we feel depleted with little to give and we force it. I am not saying that you shouldn't share your last dollar or meal, but that there needs to be a balance between giving and receiving. If you are feeling that you have nothing to give concentrate on receiving for a while until you gain some strength. You can also give in ways that would not constitute depletion such as smiling at someone when they need validation, or telling someone that you love them.

CHAPTER SIX

Escape/Relaxation

Sleeping, napping, funny movies, laughing, meditation, praying, reading, watching television, going to the movies, daydreaming, thinking about the past and future.

For most of us, relaxing is pleasurable. Activities that help us escape are many times considered pleasurable activities and provide us with rest from our day-to-day overloads. People state that they need to relax because of the stress they experience. Our bodies regenerate and heal from stressors when we relax.[134] Relaxing helps us *escape* from our everyday lives. Although escape is often perceived as a bad thing, escape is necessary in order to fight feelings of constriction, hopelessness, or exhaustion. When we escape we can refuel energies, thoughts, and feelings.

Escaping also provides us with a venue in which to process thoughts. Many great thinkers have constructed their most illuminating and creative ideas when they have taken a break, or escaped, from their studies or investigations. Escaping provides us with the time and space that we need to process events or thoughts without pressure. Relieving the pressure we feel allows for more creativity and solutions to problems.

Having highlighted the importance of escaping, I must also add that many times, although not all the time, it is important not to escape from our feelings. When I get bombarded by a feeling that makes me crazy, such as lack of control or incompetence, I automatically go into "doing mode." I engage in some sort of activity to drive me away from the feelings I am experiencing. For a brief period of time this is healthy, but after a while the unresolved issues come back.

What I try to do now is to acknowledge the feeling, feel it, sit with it, and do nothing to try to change it. I don't try to find meaning in it (another way to escape) or try to find a way to change it. I just sit, observe, and feel. Most of the time, these negative feelings subside in a matter of minutes. Sometimes they resurface again, but I know that they come and go and that I can simply witness them.

Sleeping/Napping/Daydreaming

Scholars repeatedly document that we need to sleep well. Getting enough sleep maximizes our happiness. Not getting enough sleep predisposes us to multiple cognitive, emotional, physical and spiritual ailments.[135,136] Dr. Nilesh Dave, medical director of the Sleep and Breathing Disorders Center at University of Texas Southwestern Medical Centre, states that a lack of sleep contributes to depression, anxiety, obesity, sexual dysfunction, relationship discord, etc.[137]

Sleep gives us the opportunity to escape, relax, and recharge. A high level of stress is argued to correlate with low levels of sleep.[20,138]

Although most people accept the fact that getting enough sleep is important and influences mood, napping carries some stigma, especially in the United States. Napping doesn't adhere to our over work practices and people believe that those who nap are lazy. Although many people around the world nap as part of their routine, for Americans, napping is a luxury that does not lead to success and productivity. Researchers disagree and state that napping rejuvenates, helps creativity, and makes one more productive. As a matter of fact, many great thinkers have used naps as a time for inspiration and insight.

Daydreaming is also stigmatized as a non-productive activity performed only by those who are lazy, have nothing else to do, or have trouble concentrating. Scholars propose that daydreaming provides for a time where one can indulge in practicing what may happen in the future without repercussions. For example, you can daydream about how your new furniture will look without buying anything. You can daydream about quitting your job before actually quitting. Daydreaming provides one with the chance to play out possibilities in life before committing to them.

In addition, visualization (daydreaming) is a popular activity in the self-development field. Therapists instruct

---

[20] Low levels of sleep can cause stress as stress can cause problems in sleeping. One factor can feed of another creating a feedback loop.

their clients to imagine what they want as a way to get it. Visualization is a way to keep one on track towards one's goals. It also provides for a way to change self-perceptions. Visualizing that one is strong and confident, for example, helps one to believe and act as strong and confident.

Whether one finds pleasure in dreaming, napping, or daydreaming, all are often reported as pleasurable and can lead to increased happiness.

Spirituality/ Meditation

People find pleasure in meditative activities such as sitting on a cushion, running, or praying. Pleasure is experienced when we meditate because it brings us to another state of being. In a meditative state, your sense of self and your environment is altered. People have stated the following about meditation:

> *"I feel like my body is coming apart; I am being flipped upside down"*[139]
>
> *"Meditation is like an everlasting orgasm"*[140]
>
> *"Out of body experience"*[141]

Meditation has been described as "the best natural high" and has been reported to provide a feeling of "restful, silent, and of heightened alertness."[142] Scholars say that it promotes clarity, sense of connection, energy, mood, and calmness.[143] Dr. Bloomfield, author of *TM-Transcendental Meditation*, argues that meditation incites enjoyment in life, especially in daily routines. Meditation practices promote the slowing down of life in order to find pleasures in moments or experiences. Dr. Bloomfield states that his patients report having more enjoyment in life after beginning the practice of meditation.[144]

Sitting on a cushion and keeping your mind blank most often achieves a meditative state, but there are other activities that are also meditative, such as running or painting. Mihaly Csíkszentmihályi, author of *Flow*, writes about flow activities. When you are in the flow, time stands stills and you loose consciousness of your environment. Csíkszentmihályi relates that those who experience flow activities are the happiest. In the same manner, religious practices are declared to provide for altered states of being and to have a positive relationship to happiness.[145,146]

Laughter/Humor

Most people would agree that a good laugh helps you relax, forget about your problems, and see life in a different way. Laughter gives us positive interpretations of stressful events and helps us to become optimistic and hopeful. We use humor as a way to cope with life stressors. In this manner, humor is therapeutic and good for our well-being.[147,148]

Humor produces positive emotions and moods[149] and it decreases the impact of negative life events on affect.[150,151] Stressors become less damaging when one engages in humor. Laughing provides a form of "safety-valve" that releases pent up stress.[152]

Laughing is cited by most as pleasurable. Happiness is often measured by how often one smiles and laughs. Whether the reasons that we experience pleasure when we laugh are because it releases stress or because it connects us to others, laughter remains medicine for the soul.

Books/TV/Movies

Films and books evoke emotions that help to create feelings of hope and encouragement. They provide a space for "emotional catharsis." Some movies make us question our beliefs and practices, while others validate the same.[153] Movies and books provide us with a deeper understanding and alternate solutions to the way we live.[154,155]

We also watch movies or read books in order to escape and dream about an ideal life. The dreaming usually includes ways to change our present circumstances. Watching a movie is pleasurable because it provides us with "utopian dreams and energies." Philosopher Ernst Bloch discussed that engaging in escape is useful in creating change, especially social change.

Movies and books "animate" us by giving us hope for a better life. All forms of art, according to Bloch, contain some form of emancipatory action (literature, art, theater, music). In other words, escape through pleasure is necessary in resisting or saying "no" to our reality and in creating change. Many pleasures such as daydreaming, fashion, art, listening to music, and fantasy allow us to resist and change our realities. When we resist our realities we create opportunities for change.

Synchronicity

Carl Jung described synchronicity as "the experience of two or more events, that appear to be unrelated or unlikely to occur together by chance, that are observed to occur together in a meaningful manner."[156] People state that events that are synchronized are pleasurable such as getting a phone call from someone you were just about to call, catching someone looking at you at the exact time you looked at them, and having someone complete your sentences.

Other synchronized pleasurable events may be recalled as lucky occurrences such as being in a rush and finding all the traffic lights green, or receiving an unexpected sum of money, or having a song end exactly at the same time you reach your destination.

Synchronized events give us the opportunity to contemplate that there is more to life than what we know and see. As Carolyn North stated in *Synchronicity: The Anatomy of Coincidence*, "people love mysterious things, and synchronicity is like magic happening to them."[157] Events that are synchronized or give us luck provide us with a sense of hope that something or someone is watching over us.

To attempt to engage in more synchronized events would be paradoxical. The only thing we can do to make sure that we maximize pleasure from synchronized events is to be open to them and to look for them. We can open our minds to the possibility that life has more to offer than what we can understand and witness. With an open mind, we become privy to more synchronized events in our lives from which we derive pleasure.

Positivity

People report that thinking about positive things gives them pleasure (e.g. how grateful you are about something, how good a person is, something exciting happening). Not surprisingly, researchers have noted that happy people tend to have more positive thoughts and dispositions than those who are not as happy. Happy people see the good before they see the bad. Happy people believe in themselves, others, and the world. How positive a person is reflects how happy they are. Positivity is not only an indicator of happiness but it also can increase happiness. The more positive you can become, the happier you will be.

Happy people have more positive attitudes towards themselves and others.[158] For example, one research study reported that a higher level of positivity was related to being less self-critical.[159] Another study found a relationship between hostility and positivity. The researchers found that happy people were less likely to be hostile towards other people.[160] [161]

In the book, *Positivity*, Dr. Fredrickson has proposed a broaden-and-build theory. She argues that positivity helps us build resources. Negativity, on the other hand, although necessary at times, restricts our access to resources (such as friendships, jobs, knowledge, skills). The more we experience positivity, the more we are open to new experiences and people. Fredrickson suggests a 3-to-1 positivity ratio for optimal happiness – three positive experiences to every negative experience.[162]

Researchers warn that positivity is not about getting rid of the negative or making pretend everything is good. It is not about suppressing feelings or getting rid of all negative experiences. Both positive and negative experiences, thoughts, and feelings are valuable to our growth and well-being. What scholars argue for is experiencing more positivity than negativity.

One way to experience more positivity is by finding positive reasons for why things happen. Researchers have found that people who attribute positive understandings to events or actions are happier.[163] Dr. Fredrickson suggests that you ask what is going right or what is good right now? The answers to these questions should shed light as to the positive aspects of an event or interaction. They should also give you pleasure as people report that thinking in positive ways is pleasurable.

Other ways researchers have found to increase positivism is through gratitude. Scholars have reported that those who are the most grateful are the happiest. Emmons & McCullough from University of California and the University of Miami divided undergraduate students enrolled in a health psychology class into three intervention groups. One of the interventions included writing down on a daily basis things for which they were grateful. The results showed that the students in the gratitude group had greater increases in positive affect, pro-social behavior, life satisfaction, optimism, and connection to others than the other intervention groups.[164]

CHAPTER SEVEN

Physical

Taking a shower, getting into a warm bed, dancing, taking your shoes off at the end of the day, sunbathing, sexuality, eating, touch, massage, exercise, rocking in a hammock, dancing, masturbation, pornography, sports.

Many people describe pleasure as it relates to physical sensations. Physical sensations most often include touch, smell, motion, and taste.[21] Many therapeutic modalities are focused on getting in touch with the physical

---

[21] Sight and smell can also create physical sensations such as a racing heart when you observe a beautiful painting or smell your lover's perfume.

sensations in our bodies. Attending to physical sensations has been shown to increase physical and emotional well-being.[165,166,167]

Physical sensations leading to pleasure can be had in different ways. One is through direct touch to the body (massage, kissing, hugging, and sex). The other is through motion of the body (rocking, swaying, cruising, sexuality, exercise, thrill seeking). And the last is through ingestion into the body (aroma and food).

Touch

Physical sensations are often felt on the skin. The feeling of touch on one's skin is often cited as pleasurable. Examples can involve touch with another person, such as getting a massage. Or it can involve touch with our environment, such as feeling the wind blow through your hair or walking barefoot on the grass.

Touch is so important that scholars have noted that a lack of touch can impair brain development and even lead to death. Studies performed with orphaned babies concluded that a lack of touch was responsible for their frequent demise.

Touch, especially through the use of massage therapy, has been documented to reduce depression, pain, stress, aggression and physical ailments and to increase communication, attentiveness, competency, and immune conditions.[168,169,170] Touch helps us feel secure and helps us face adversity. Research studies have shown that touch from a loved one results in better reaction to stressful situations. Touch is also reported to relieve pain.[171]

Rocking/Motion

Researchers state that rocking in a chair, being on a boat, swinging on a swing, or swaying in a hammock relieves physical and emotional ailments. Rocking is argued to be an activity that relieves stress, fear, pain, loneliness, and anger. It has also been documented to heal heart attacks, strokes, arthritis, colds, diabetes, and cancer.[172] Rocking is a soothing technique that is practiced universally in different ways.[173] Rocking produces reactions in the body such as lowered blood pressure and slowing of respiration.[174] These physical reactions tap into the pleasure centers in the brain and produce endorphins that make the body feel pleasured.[175]

The pleasure we feel when we are in motion be it in a car or a train may be related to rocking and may have the same benefits. People often report being in motion as pleasurable. Being in motion — be it by rocking, swaying, or cruising is pleasurable and should be considered when managing pleasure.

Sexuality

The research appears to be at odds on deciding whether sexual activity (in terms of quantity) influences happiness or not. Some suggest that sexual activity or preference does not influence happiness.[176,177] The sexual activity of college students, for example, from "the most free and experienced to the most conservative and inexperienced," showed no relationship to happiness.[178,179] Other scholars report an influence of sexual activity on happiness.[180]

However, scholars believe that sexual adjustment has a stronger influence on happiness than sexual orientation or sexual activity.[181] Happy people report less sexual difficulties in their relationships.[182] When sex is good, it can increase physical and emotional well-being.[183] Healthy sexual adjustment can be found in any type and quantity of sexual activity. Hence, one can be happier if one is sexually well adjusted whether one is having no sex or having many sexual encounters.

Perhaps it is more interesting to discuss sexuality as something that is more than the sexual act. Sexuality involves being sexual and/or sensual throughout the day, not only in sexual encounters. Sexuality can be a part of any and many every-day moments. People who feel sexual or sensual walk differently and talk differently; they exude a feeling of pleasure and sensuality. The secret is getting to the point where you are feeling frequent moments of sexuality and sensuality. Your physical appearance matters a lot in this domain.[22] You want to get to the point that you feel really good inside your body; that you feel beautiful and full of sensuality.

Exercise/Sports

It is reported by researchers that exercisers are happier than non-exercisers. Exercise contributes to physical and emotional well-being, including sexual functioning. People who exercise regularly are at much lower risk of depression and anxiety than those who do not.[184,185,186,187]

Clinical trials show that exercise can effectively treat depression.[188,189] Exercise actually changes the brain. Like an antidepressant, it increases the activity of brain chemicals like serotonin and dopamine. It also releases endorphins. Exercise increases memory, concentration and clarity of thinking.[190] Tai chi and Yoga have been

---

[22] This does not mean conforming to dominant standards of beauty but to feeling good inside your own skin.

reported to strengthen the immune system and reduce blood pressure. Dancing is reported to be "one of the most powerful (and primal) ways to release endorphins."[191] Involvement in club sports has also been documented to provide for positive social and mental outcomes.[192,193]

Dr. Dennis Lobstein at the University of New Mexico compared sedentary men to men who jogged. The sedentary men were more depressed and had lower levels of endorphins than the joggers. Dr. Thayer at California State University found that exercise was reported to be the most effective activity in changing a bad mood when they studied people in changing a bad mood.[194]

I don't have to tell you to exercise; the media is full of messages regarding this topic.[23] I am merely documenting that exercise appears to be an integral component to happiness. For many of us exercise is a natural high and a source of tremendous pleasure. The secret is to find something you enjoy doing. After all, there is no point in doing something you don't like. The point is to increase pleasurable activities in order to maximize well-being.

Eating/Cooking

Food is a universal pleasure. Eating makes you feel good; food gives you pleasure. Mother nature has made eating food pleasurable in order to ensure that we survive.

We feel good when we eat, but we also need to eat to feel good. Some researchers suggest that increasing the

---

[23] Exercise has different definitions. For one person it may be going to the gym, for another it may mean gardening or dancing. The point is to move your body regularly in more ways than getting in your car.

nutrients in our diet will increase our emotional and physical well-being. Scholars have indicated that a lack of nutrients such as calcium, iron, folic acid, magnesium, etc. is correlated to cognitive and emotional ailments such as depression, anxiety, etc. Likewise, fast-food eaters have higher stress levels than those who are not.[195]

We can get used to eating any type of food. Some of us become vegetarians and never miss eating meat, while others find immense pleasure in eating meat. The pleasure we receive is related to what experiences we have had. If one has only eaten ground beef, one does not know the pleasure of eating steak. Hence, eating ground beef can be as pleasurable as eating steak.

In the end, it doesn't really matter what we eat but how we eat it. The French, for example, are famous for savoring their food. Eating is an art for them. The food that is eaten whether it is a carrot or a t-bone is given special status. Hence, the pleasure in its consumption is heightened. Also, foods are not ingested in the same exact way day after day. If carrots are the food of choice, they are cooked in different ways every time. The experience of eating these carrots is heightened, prolonged, and manipulated. Eating is an art for the French because it is seen as pleasurable part of life rather than a necessity.

In *Elements of Taste*, Kunz and Kaminsky argue that time is an integral part of the dining experience and one needs to prolong the moment and savor it.[196] Food becomes an occasion to be shared with family and friends. Rushing is not a good thing.

Italians are also well known for the attention they give to pleasure and food. The average Italian meal is three hours long, for example. Next time you eat, put the food in your mouth and eat it slowly. Be mindful to the taste and the texture.[197] Some refer to this as deep tasting and it "involves full attention" to food.[198]

The sense of taste is accompanied other senses such as sight and smell. Eating should be a multisensory experience if pleasure is to be heightened. Take away sight and your pleasure is diminished.[24] Hence, set up a beautiful table or put on beautiful music and the pleasure you experience while eating will be maximized.

Sensation Seeking

Researchers have noted that happy people tend to engage in more exciting activities than people who are not as happy. It has been stated that sensation seekers are happier.[199] Exciting experiences can be categorized as sensation seeking. Sensation seeking activities have been defined as varied, novel, intense, and somewhat risky such as: parachuting, snowboarding, white water rafting, hang-gliding, bungee jumping, rock climbing, motorcycling, SCUBA diving and racecar driving. Any person who can be described in the following ways is believed to be a sensation-seeking person:[200]

- Thrill and adventure seeking (engaging in risky physical activities)
- Experience seeking (seeking new experience through mind and sensation)
- Disinhibited (partying, social drinking, sex)
- Susceptible to boredom (aversion for unchanging or unstimulating environments or persons)

---

[24] For those who have are not able to see for prolonged periods of time, sensations in other areas are maximized. Or if one blindfolds someone when eating, their taste sensations should be heightened.

If we engage in an unpredictable experience, we activate part of our brain (the reward circuitry) that rewards us with good feelings (pleasure, happiness, or satisfaction). Both negative (being punished) and positive (being kissed) experiences activate the same part of the brain[201][202] because pleasure is felt when dopamine levels are released. Dopamine is dispensed, as the body gets ready to act to a new event. It doesn't matter whether the event is good or bad.[203] Dopamine helps the body to act as it signals to the body that something important is about to happen (anticipation).

Some of us are more open to sensation producing experiences than others. Sensation seekers have high thresholds for intense auditory and visual stimulation.[204] They also tend to engage in more drug use, sexually risky behaviors, and violence.[205] The goal of the sensation seeker is to increase arousal.[206] Some researchers argue that high sensation seekers have "stimulus hunger"[207] and produce low levels of dopamine.[208]

Why do some of us need more sensation than others? Some say that it is hereditary, while others say that it is a need to disconnect from oneself or to avoid one's problems. Still others speculate that it may have to do with having intense stimuli while growing up.[209,210]

Most of the time we perceive people who take risks as irresponsible. However, these types of people are usually the creators of new ideas and ways of doing things.[211] They are the explorers in society.

The bottom line is that sensation-producing activities can be a source of great pleasure. It is beneficial to think about which activities in this category you may want to incorporate into your life.

CHAPTER EIGHT

Mastery

Solving a puzzle, fixing something, dialogue, reading a book, getting out of a difficult situation, creation, learning, completing something, getting an award, getting a promotion, taking a class, going to the library, surfing the internet

Mastery is defined as "the mysterious process during which what is at first difficult becomes progressively easier and more pleasurable through practice."[212] George Leonard, author of *Mastery: The Keys to Success and Long-Term Fulfillment*, states that mastery is available to everyone. Mastery involves time and dedication and one is often faced with frustration and impatience. We experience pleasure when we overcome obstacles and challenges, whether that be getting someone to fall in love with you, or becoming successful when you have been deemed to be stupid, or finishing a report. Overcoming the difficult and the unlikely fuels our pleasure cells.

Leonard states that mastery is a process involving many ups, downs, and plateaus and that the key to maximizing pleasure is to engage in the activity for the sake of engagement and not for the sake of mastery. In that way, you find pleasure in both the ups and the downs of the process and not merely in the resolution of the activity.

The mastery process involves creation, learning, completion, and recognition.

Creation

Creation is frequently reported to be pleasurable, such as figuring out a way to make something work better, discussing and generating new ideas, making a sculpture, thinking of an idea for a book, etc.

Most often we attribute the process of creation to artists (writers, painters, crafters, cooks). Images of the ill- fated artists who are dark, mysterious, and miserable come to mind when we think of the creative process. Many times we think that creativity is only for those who are miserable or that the creative process is a passionate and desolate process. I don't know if happy people are more creative than those who are less happy, but I do know that creativity brings more happiness to most people, whether they are miserable or happy.

Although we think that creativity belongs to artists, there are many activities that are not considered artistic that are creative (science, philosophy, business, mechanics, event planning, etc.). Creation involves innovation, change, and progress.[213] The act of being creative involves deriving pleasure from the "process of problem-solving."[214,215,216] Finding a solution to a problem gives one a sense of mastery and control. The "problem" could be finding a new way to think about something, or finding a new way to wash your clothes, or building a new house, or fixing an old radio, or getting out of a situation that is difficult.

The creative process many times includes a moment where one feels suspended in time and place. Consciousness is transformed to a meditative state. As previously discussed, meditative states are a source of great pleasure because of their ability to produce life-altering experiences.

Learning

Learning is a byproduct as well as an instrument of the mastery process. You have to engage in learning in order to master, but you also learn in mastering. Learning is achieved in many different domains and involves cognitive, physical and emotional lessons. We can learn a new vocabulary word (cognitive), or a new way to make pasta (physical), or how to let go of control in moments of stress (emotional).

Learning is pleasurable because it provides us with innovation. When we learn, another world opens up for us to explore. Learning is also pleasurable because it usually means it will get us something or somewhere else. Learning usually leads us to getting things such as a new job, friends, or activities.

We all learn in different ways and in different domains (cognitive, emotional, physical). Sometimes it is difficult to value our learning experiences because they differ from what the majority of people experience as learning. For example, I spend a tremendous amount of time learning emotionally. First of all, people cannot perceive that I'm learning in this domain as readily as if I were learning to drive. Also, people may not value this type of learning over other types such as learning history or learning to garden. Hence, it is important that you understand that people learn in different ways and different types of things and that learning is an integral part of happiness and pleasure and that you have justification in its pursuit, regardless of whether or not it falls under the category of customary or normal.

Completion

Completing a challenging experience is a sweet feeling. What can be more pleasurable than getting or doing what everyone has thought to be difficult, if not impossible? Completions of less challenging processes are also pleasurable such as washing the dishes or finishing a report. Setting up your life in order to assure that you experience completion of activities is a good idea if you want to maximize pleasure.

Many self-development coaches prescribe that you allocate more time than you think it will take to complete a task so that you can ensure that it will be completed. In that way, you set yourself up for success in the completion of things and hence, create more opportunities for pleasure.

Although completion is a source of great satisfaction, it could also be a source of great limitation. I know many people who determine their self-worth on how often they complete things. They always finish what they start. In my opinion, there are start-ups that are better not finished than finished. The point is that sometimes we can become so involved in the end result, "it is good to complete things" that we become inflexible and cannot see a greater good, "this is not working, let me try something else."

Recognition

Pleasurable experiences most often include those that involve recognition for our mastery. Examples are a promotion, a good grade, a compliment, etc. The fact that we enjoy recognition should encourage us to get involved in an environment that it is conducive to recognition.

Receiving recognition is a tricky process. Recognition does not necessarily mean that one has performed well. Or, to be clearer, non-recognition does not necessarily mean that one has performed badly. Recognition largely depends on the quantity and quality of the people that surround you. If people who do not value your work surround you, you will never receive recognition no matter how well you perform.

The point I am making is that it is important to be surrounded by the right sort of people if you are to maximize pleasure in the area of mastery and recognition. It means being surrounded by people who appreciate and nurture your work. Make it a priority to find people who value you in order to maximize pleasure in your life.

CHAPTER NINE

Environment

Looking at the moon, going to the beach, swimming in a lake, going for a walk, sound, breeze, warm weather, mornings, rain, cleaning, organizing, gardening

Activities having to do with one's surroundings are often noted to be pleasurable, such as being in nature, arranging flowers, the sound of music, or gardening. We find pleasure in incents, waterfalls, music, wind chimes, soaps, candles, fire, paintings, furniture, etc. Similarly, we clean and organize so that our homes are comfortable and peaceful.

Physical surroundings influence physical and

emotional well-being.[217,218,219] We sometimes ignore what surrounds us when living day-to-day. We don't realize how influential light, color, cleanliness, smell, and sound are to our moods. Environments can increase positive affect and inhibit negative thoughts.[220] Environments can provide for stress reduction, emotion regulation and increased positive feelings. Research has shown that physical surroundings are conducive to restorative experiences.[221] Research conducted in hospitals and in work settings showed that having a sunny room, using color, or having art and plants helps people to heal and be more productive.[222,223,224] People are reported to feel "safer and calmer."

Home/Domestic Life

Our homes are a source of great respite for us and we should try to make these surroundings pleasurable. Our homes are meant to make us feel safe, relaxed and comfortable. Home is usually were one can regenerate and release stress.[225]

The way our homes look and smell influence our well-being. Domestic activities that contribute to a beautiful and peaceful home are often noted to be pleasurable such as cleaning or having flowers in a vase. Having an organized home and having beautiful things to look at is pleasurable for many.

Nature

People repeatedly state that spending time in nature is pleasurable. They mention the beach, the woods, swimming in a lake, walking in the rain, looking at a rainbow, or basking under a moonlit sky. Being in nature contributes to mood stabilization. One research study showed that when people looked at a landscape scene, they reported less anxiety or stress and needed less pain medication than those who did not.[226]

Scholars have argued that the disconnection we have with nature has contributed to many psychological and emotional problems.[227] Among other things, this research has shown that contact with nature and natural elements can reduce anxiety, lower blood pressure, and lessen pain.[228,229,230]

For many, enjoyment of nature leads to a sense of spirituality and an appreciation for powers larger than oneself. We realize that we are part of a larger whole, which reduces some of the stress we feel. It gives us comfort and purpose.

Therapists use time in nature as a therapeutic intervention through which to increase well-being.[231] Contact with nature is prescribed as a way to heal emotional ailments.[232]

Light/Color

Color and lighting are important components in physical surroundings. The lack of sunlight or daylight has been shown to lead to illnesses such as Seasonal Affective Disorder.[233] People who are exposed every day to high levels of natural sunlight are at less risk for depression.[234] In her book, *Positivity*, Dr. Fredrickson told of a study done by one of her graduate students where he found that people who spent twenty minutes or more outside had more of an increase in positivity than those who did not.[235] Bright light stimulates the brain's production of serotonin. Serotonin is a neurotransmitter that helps the brain's depressive stress response. Exposure to daylight in healthcare settings has been associated with positive health outcomes such as reduced length of stay, medication intake, and depression.[236]

Color is important in the regulation of mood. Chromotherapy, or color therapy, is the term used for therapeutic interventions using color. Chromotherapists apply color and light to the body in order to help it heal. Color is argued to restore balance to the body. Sometimes I prescribe that patients do the following exercise to reduce stress or anxiety. It is often referred to as "color breathing" or "color visualization" and is used to treat cancer patients.

Exercise: Color Breathing
Sit or lie in a comfortable position. Close your eyes and imagine the color that is most soothing to you at that moment. Breathe in slowly and deeply as you think of this color. Feel the color enter your body with each breath. Imagine the color touching every part of your body. Imagine that the color surrounds you and that you inhale and exhale that color. You can perform this exercise for anywhere from 5 minutes to 20 minutes. You can help yourself to visualize color by looking at the color before hand.

Aroma

The use of aroma to ameliorate physical and emotional ailments has been around for 6,000 years. Aromatherapy uses essential oils to combat depression, anxiety, fatigue, anger, stress, to name a few. Researchers have documented the success of infusing aroma in increasing positive mood and reducing physical and emotional pain.[237,238]

Similar to color, Aromatherapists will frequently observe that their clients are instinctively drawn toward the essential oil that is right for their needs.

Sound/Music

Research has documented the ill effect of noise on patient outcomes. Noise increases stress.[239] There are sounds that impact us so much that we feel it change the composition of our bodies and moods. The sound of a honking horn, someone yelling, a screeching car, and alarms can accelerate our heart beat, make us sweat, and make us feel anxious, angry, and confused. Sound affects us psychologically, physically, cognitively, and behaviorally.

On the other hand, there is overwhelming evidence that music alters mood in a positive way.[240,241] Music changes our physical and emotional states. Music helps us sleep and reduces anxiety, depression, pain, stress, developmental disorders, traumatic brain injury, etc.[242]

I don't think we need researchers to tell us that sound alters mood or that it can be therapeutic. We know that when we listen to a song that is upbeat and fast, it makes us peppier and happier. The same happens when we listen to relaxing and tranquil tunes; our bodies become relaxed. Sound is vibration and every part of our bodies feels the vibration, even our cells. Joshua Leads in *The Power of Sound* says that "sound touches us and influences our emotion like no other source of input." He writes that everything has a particular resonant frequency and that we are attracted to things (even colors) and people that have the same sound frequency as we do.

Building Your Enviroscape

It is important that we acknowledge and incorporate sounds, sights, and smells that resonate well with us so that we don't create a "nervous system friction" or an imbalance in what you need and what you have coming into your body. Notice the sounds, aromas, and sights around you in order to eliminate the ones that are irritating and enhance the ones that are pleasurable. You are probably attracted to particular sounds, aromas and objects, and colors. Incorporate them into your daily life because the attraction has been argued to be reflective of what you need emotionally and physically.

PART III

PUTTING PLEASURE INTO ACTION

The happiness scholars focus on genetics, context, and activities as components to happiness. I believe that there is one other component that has not received enough attention in the scholarly literature. I have labeled this component as "Resolve." Dr. Fordyce found that after all is said and done happy people are just more invested in happiness than others.

However, our reality is that pleasure is not valued and that most of us have not resolved to be happy. We value work over happiness and participate in over-work activities. The valuing of work over happiness gets in the way of a joyous and pleasurable life. The irony is that I believe many of us would change our work habits if we had enough information regarding happiness and well-being.

Having stated this, I have to declare that if anyone had told me a few months back that I needed to decide to be happy, I would have told him or her to "fuck off." I was in a state of despair and deep sadness. I felt that a decision to be happy was beyond my circumstances. At that point in time, I could not make a decision like this. However, after increasing pleasurable activities, I did get to the point of being able to decide to be happy. I could never have gotten to the point of decision without first modifying my behavior.

What I am trying to say is that there are two factors in happiness, one being behavior (pleasurable activities) and one being cognition/emotion (resolve). We need both in order to lead a joyful life. Sometimes we cannot resolve to be happy without first changing our behavior because we are in so much pain that we cannot think clearly enough to make any decision.

The previous part of this book focused on increasing pleasurable activities, the next part focuses on committing to happiness and pleasure and addressing obstacles. You may think that it is easy to incorporate pleasure into your life, but many times it is difficult. The more you create a network that supports your new lifestyle and the more you can anticipate the obstacles you will face, the better results you will get.

CHAPTER TEN

Beyond Activity

Some pursue happiness – others create it. Unknown[243]

Some researchers have argued that happiness does not come from what we have but from how we feel. Happiness does not come from the outside (i.e. where we live, what we do, or who we date), but rather from the inside (how satisfied we are with ourselves). I agree and disagree. As I stated previously, I believe happiness is derived from our actions (engaging in pleasurable activities) and our feelings and thoughts.

The day I passed my final examination for my Ph.D., I was pretty happy. The happiness lasted about one day. I quickly forgot about my huge accomplishment and my sense of good fortune. Life went back to what it had always been.

You would think that I would have engaged in some fun and pleasure after having passed my exam. Nope, I decided that I couldn't just yet — that it wasn't the right time — that I needed to finish a book first. I thought I didn't have enough money or time and that I needed to work on getting my life perfected. So, I worked and worked until the day I got really sad. This was the day that I realized how inconsequential everything I would achieve would be in my life in comparison to how much I was enjoying life.

More of something outside of myself (such as finishing a book, graduating, or having a nicer body) was not going to allow me to feel pleasure. I realized that day that it didn't matter how much money I had, how many books I had written, or how many degrees I had. All that mattered was that I wanted to feel vibrant inside; that I wanted to feel alive inside. I knew I could have these things NOW!

But I couldn't find a way to start feeling vibrant. What was I to do? What was I to think in order to feel vibrant, joyful, and full of a pleasurable life? I didn't even know where to begin. I just couldn't feel it inside of me. How do you get to feeling like you are actually enjoying life?

I had to decide that this was actually something I wanted now and that I wasn't willing to wait any longer. That's it — just a decision. At that moment I closed the computer, got out of bed, and went for a really long walk.

Resolve

Happiness is more than adding pleasures to your life and then stirring the pot. Happiness is about exuding a pleasurable state of being. It is about becoming a person who radiates energy and that truly enjoys life. It is about being open and wanting to live life fully. And finally, it is about enjoying life now and not waiting until later.

Happy people are committed to their happiness and pleasure. Happy people value and give time and attention to their happiness. Researchers have demonstrated that happy people want happiness more than others. Happy people are invested in happiness, pleasure, and living life to its fullest; they are invested in a vibrant life. Pleasure is part of their life purpose. Dr. Fordyce suggests that you attempt to live your live as if happiness is your top priority for a month in order to get an idea of how happy people live.

> *"Interestingly enough, it appears that the people that are the happiest seem to be the ones who simply want it the most."*[244]

Committing to happiness and pleasure is a necessary part of maximizing happiness. I have a friend who routinely complains about the bad luck she has. She repeats over and over again how unhappy she is with what she has. To be fair, she does have reason to say that she has bad luck and that her life is not the best that she deserves. She is like many of us that are dealt with a life less than spectacular. I have told my friend, as I tell you now, that an important step to becoming happy, aside from engaging in pleasurable activities, is to decide to be happy.

There was a time in my life when I felt excruciating emotional pain. I could have remained in pain, but instead I decided to get down on my knees and repeat to myself, "I want to be happy; I want to be happy." I knew that until I decided that I wanted to be happy, I would be unhappy.

I am convinced that life provides us with endless opportunities including one of leading a life that is full of vitality, hope, and zest. You must get to the point that you know with all certainty that you can have the life that you desire. Until you are convinced that you can have it all, you won't be able to get it. Many people ask me, "but if I can have it all then that means that everyone can have it all, and the reality is that we can't all have it all." This is true given the world we live in now. There are so many people suffering and so many forms of injustice, but that doesn't mean that the world should remain this way. This does not mean that the world cannot get better and better as it gets older.

I see it as my duty to be happy and optimistic because when I am, I am contributing to a better world. If we truly want to fight social injustice we need to become whole within ourselves. There is no use in fighting battles to end poverty or cruelty if one is not happy, because in a state of unhappiness, we are not at our best and may treat others unjustly. If you want a better world where most of us are happy most of the time then it is your duty to become happy.

Everything in this book is meaningless unless you decide to be happy. Sometimes making this decision is not easy and you may need to engage in some behavioral changes first. After you incorporate some pleasurable activities into your life, you can think about making a decision to be happy or not.

Forcing Pleasure

If you are anything like me, you will want immediate gratification and expect to redesign your life in a matter of a few days. The truth is that it takes some time to change habits, behaviors, and attitudes. You have been sustaining and nurturing a particular life style for a very long time. To erase all those moments takes time. Self-development gurus talk about the law of gender where any creation needs an incubation period. Incubation period or gestation is dependent on the size of the tree (change) you plan on growing. If the change you desire is large, the waiting time will be longer. In other words, time has to pass before a seed or idea moves into form.

When I first started, I wanted pleasure badly. I focused on it so hard that I became miserable when things did not go the way I planned. I felt angry and my mood was horrible. Feeling like this just made my day even worse. I realized during these first few days that I was a bit of a control freak. I even wanted to control pleasure. I needed to release the grip of control. I needed to let the day unfold and to find pleasure in the things that it provided. There is a fine line between planning for pleasure and letting pleasure happen spontaneously. I have found that you need a bit of both in order to maximize pleasure.

I am telling you this because as a therapist I know how important it is to be clear about expectations so that we don't sabotage our endeavors. The clearer the expectations, the less probability there is for misunderstandings, conflict, and resignation.

CHAPTER ELEVEN

Time to Begin!

It is time to start living your life of pleasure. Focusing on pleasure day-to-day is immensely satisfying but can be difficult. How can something enjoyable be difficult? As I said before, your body and mind have gotten accustomed to living in a particular way and it can be difficult to train them to engage in something different. This chapter provides you with exercises that will help you get into the mindset of feeling pleasure and happiness. It also provides tips on how to be mindful of the moments you experience in order to maximize the pleasure you experience. Finally, I discuss obstacles and give you some guidelines as to how to handle them. All in all, my goal in this chapter is to help you create an environment that will aid you in overcoming the moments of difficulty you may encounter.

Imagine Your Happiness

Before you get out of bed in the morning and before you fall asleep at night imagine what you want your happiness to **feel** like. Instead of imagining the things that you want in the future (e.g. house, car, or job), imagine what you want to feel like.

As you do this you will notice that you will begin to feel the feeling that you aspire for yourself. And feeling that feeling even for 5 minutes a day is a step in the right direction. It opens your mind and body to experience this feeling. When I first did this exercise I thought about the happiness I wanted to feel in the future. I then started to imagine what that would feel like. In a matter of minutes, I was feeling that happiness.

Begin the Day with Pleasure

A day that begins well puts into motion more goodness for the rest of the day. Identify pleasurable things you can do right after you get out of bed — don't wait until the day gets going. You may exercise, turn on some music, dance, sing in the shower, have a good breakfast, daydream about the day ahead, etc.

There have been times when I have tried starting the day with something pleasurable but something went wrong, like my coffee being bad or my child getting sick. In the past, I would have given up and this unexpected beginning would have affected my whole day. But instead, I simply start my day over. The day my coffee was bad, I waited a bit and had one that was better. Or, the day my child got sick, I changed my schedule to include pleasurable activities that involved staying in bed with her.

One important lesson I learned throughout this process is that I have to push myself to overcome difficulties. I often think of dieting when I face difficulty because in dieting one often finds a way to cheat. When you cheat, and eat a cookie, for example, you have two choices: you can either stop after the first cookie or you can say to yourself "I've had one already, I might as well have the whole box." (I've had many moments where I have eaten the whole box.)

We often allow one bad decision or event to give us an excuse to make a series of bad decisions or get involved in a series of bad moods. When I take a step back in the progress I want to make, whether it is eating a cookie on a diet or speaking to my child in a bad way, I take a moment and stop everything. I stop and become still. After I feel some stillness, I have a dialogue with myself that usually goes something like this, "you messed up but you don't need to continue to do it, you can stop here." I convince myself that I can't do anything to erase that past moment where I ate the cookie but I can do something about what I am going to do from that point on.

Mindfulness

Happy people are known for savoring life's pleasures and for living in the present moment.[245] Mindfulness "achieves a clear awareness of one's inner and outer worlds, including thoughts, emotions, sensations, actions, or surroundings as they exist at any given moment."[246] Mindfulness does not allow any thought or feeling to interfere with the moment and all that is important is witnessing the moment.

Most often our activities are influenced by our thoughts (biases, prejudices, beliefs, etc.), which result in people becoming more in touch with their thoughts than with the activity at hand. Mindfulness is about removing these filters and experiencing the moment in a "raw state." A slowing down of self and a removal of judgments is conducive to a mindful state. We may even be mindful of thoughts and feelings as we observe them rather than interact with them or react to them.

The first step in mindfulness is to slow down. I notice that I don't enjoy things if I feel rushed. When I slow down even the most rudimentary tasks become enjoyable, such as washing the dishes, driving or going to the supermarket. It's hard to shake off the feeling that there isn't enough time, especially if you don't have enough time. Sometimes, however, this feeling of exasperation is due to habit more than reality. I found myself rushing when I didn't need to. When I find myself in this state I ask myself over and over, "What are you rushing for?"

The following exercises will help you slow down and get an idea of what a mindful state feels like.

Exercise 1: Slow Motion

Next time you do something rudimentary such as going grocery shopping or brushing your teeth, make time stand still. Slow the process way down where you are actually noticing everything around you. Don't rush through the act in order to get it done. Enjoy the process of doing it. You may feel the need to rush and get through it but stop yourself every time and make yourself come in tune with the moment

Exercise 2: Swimming in Air[247]

Imagine that you are swimming underwater and have water all around you. Substitute the water for air. Feel the air all around you. Move your body as if you are in an ocean of air. Stay still and feel the air touch your body. Feel how it caresses your skin and embraces you.

Body Awareness

My life style encouraged isolation from my body. I was disconnected from my body as I rushed from moment to moment, ate junk food, watched too much T.V., did little socializing, etc. When I ran errands, my mind was always on the next thing I had to do, rather than being connected to how my body was feeling.

The more aware we are of our bodies, the more pleasure we will have. Also, the more pleasure we have, the more aware we become of our bodies. They both influence each other. The point being that attention to our bodies and the sensations in which we engage is important to our well-being. Researchers have shown that disconnection from our bodies leads to physical and emotional ailments, such as high blood pressure, anxiety, and depression.[248] I am proposing that the more pleasure we have, the more aware we will become of our bodies.

Exercise: Body Awareness

Focus your attention on your body. Become very conscious of what you are doing at this precise moment. Are you sitting? Where are you sitting? How does it feel to be sitting? Feel everything that surrounds your body such as the chair, the air, the noise, the smell, and the touch of your hands on the book or computer. Completely focus on your sensations at this exact moment. What does your mouth taste like? What is your breathing like? Slow everything down so that time seems to trickle away. Do this for one minute. You may want to give up because you want to move ahead. Most often we want to run to the next moment in order to get where we want to go and we don't savor the actual moment of living. Savoring the moment is paramount to feeling pleasure. If you bypass moments in order to get to other moments you will never feel any moment.

Flow

Csíkszentmihályi is an expert on flow experiences. He suggests that being in "flow" gives a person a deep sense of enjoyment. Flow accentuates the need for challenge. Csíkszentmihályi states that flow is achieved when one's ability is stretched and challenged to its limits. In addition, moment-by-moment enjoyment in everything we do is accentuated. Csíkszentmihályi states that just about anything can become a flow experience. You can take any activity a step further in the competency you feel and the challenge it brings. If you like listening to music, for example, you should invest some energy and time into expanding and deepening the way you listen to music. Challenge and push the limits of the experience. Think about how you can explore in a deeper and more complex way the things that give you pleasure now.

Obstacles

Any change is usually met with resistance. This resistance can come from you or from others. Anticipating the obstacles you will face when increasing pleasure in your life will help you cope with difficulties because you will be prepared. Knowing what obstacles you may encounter will give you strength and conviction about your process. Take a moment to answer the following questions in order to get an idea of potential obstacles.

1. Given your old definition of pleasure (Chapter 3), what reactions can you anticipate from others?
2. Given your old definition of pleasure, look at the types of feelings you described. Which feelings do you anticipate to be difficult?
3. Read over your new definition of pleasure. What parts of it sound different from how you live your life now?

I knew that the reactions from one side of my family would be of anger, fear, and resentment. I knew that I would probably be labeled as irresponsible. Also, I thought my friends would think I was crazy or kinky and that my professional peers would think that I was being unprofessional and not scholarly. Reading over my definitions, I knew I would have feelings of doubt, incompetence and marginalization. I knew there would be moments that I would feel totally not normal and that I would have a strong urge to comform in order to feel normal. Lastly, my old definition of pleasure indicated to me that I may encounter problems focusing on taking care of myself because I hadn't done so in the past. There are some ways to deal with obstacles:

1. Make a commitment of time — let's say 30 days. Create a 30-day challenge where any negative thought that comes into your mind, will be told to go away and replaced with a positive one.
2. Any time a negative thought gets into your head think of something for which you are grateful. As a matter of fact, you should list the things for which you feel grateful every time you go to bed and get up in the morning.
3. Write a mission or purpose statement. What kind of vibrant lifestyle do you want to have and why? Be specific. You can't get to a place you have not defined.
4. Get a friend to coach you. Tell them that they need to keep you motivated no matter what. The only thing you want to hear out of their mouth is "just finish your commitment period, you are doing great!"
5. Get yourself moving when you are feeling very defeated. I don't know how many times I have had to take a step outside of myself and say, "You will not give up; you will continue." It works because it gets you moving and then you realize that there is some hope.

Mentors

At times of doubt it is necessary to have people you can look to that have achieved what you wish for in life. They don't have to be people you know. There was a moment in this process when people said to me, "You might as well throw that Ph.D. out the window with this talk about pleasure."

They felt that being a scholar did not include talking about pleasure, especially when I talked about sensuality and sexuality. They felt that writing a book that was meant for many different types of people and not the academic world was reflective of my lack of scholarly aptitude. I asked myself, "Why can't I be a scholar and have a fun and be sexual?" or "Why can't scholars be on YouTube and write in simple language?" I will never forget the day when a group of female doctoral students walked together to class and one of them said to me, "Marisol, you shouldn't wear the long earrings you wear, you won't be taken seriously."

I knew that I was charting new territory and that this meant that I would have to face resistance. There were many moments where I felt doubtful that I was doing the right thing. There were many moments were I was at the point of quitting. But I found a mentor. My mentor was not a scholar but an entertainer. I know this will help some people to view me in an even less scholarly way, but she helped me get out of times of doubt. My mentor was Shakira. Shakira embodied the type of person I would like to be. From what I gathered, Shakira has been able to be sexual/sensual and popular (reaching all types of audiences) while still providing quality messages and being a strong manager of her business. She is also known to be very smart and educated. So, I watched video after video of Shakira until I felt I could go on.

Pleasure Log

The following table may be helpful in determining the areas in which you are often engaging in pleasure and the areas that need more attention. It also gives you an indication as to your mood as you engage in these activities. For each day, check off the activities in which you engage. Also note your mood with a number from one to five (1= worst mood to 5= the best mood).

	Date	Date	Date	Date
OVERALL MOOD				
Social Connection				
Validation/Belonging				
Self-Grooming				
Intimacy and Love				
Giving Back				
Escape/Relaxation				
Sleeping/Napping/Daydreaming				
Spirituality/Meditation				
Laughter/Humor				
Books/TV/Movies				
Positivity				
Physical/Sensory				
Touch				
Sexuality				
Sensation Seeking				
Exercise				
Eating/Cooking				
Mastery				
Creation				
Learning				
Completion				
Recognition				
Environment				
Home/Domestic Life				
Nature				
Light/Color				
Aroma				
Sound/Music				

AFTERWORD

Attending to pleasure has been a real challenge for me because I am the type of person that is always giving to others and putting myself second. To begin to think about my happiness and the pleasure I had in my life was difficult because it meant that I sometimes had to put my needs and desires first. When I started to think about pleasure I realized that I was pulled in so many directions by other people's needs that I didn't have time for what I needed. It made me feel rushed, hassled, scattered, angry and taken for granted. It was difficult to focus on myself and I had to fight an overwhelming feeling of guilt. I felt that if I didn't make other people happy, that I would lose them.

These are my personal obstacles and yours will probably be different. The point being is that you may face difficulty when attending to pleasure. In the end, similar to my experience, I hope that this process gives you insight as to yourself and your relationship to others. It is truly eye awakening. My wish for you is that you gain as much from this as I have gained. And, of course, that your happiness or well-being is increased and that you find a way to lead a joyous, vibrant and pleasurable life!

APPENDIX

LIST OF PLEASURES[249]

SOCIAL

- Making others laugh
- Having an interesting conversation
- Making a new friend
- Meeting someone you really like
- Having people that love you
- Finding out others experience the same problems
- Having your friend save you a seat
- Flirting
- Feeling like you belong somewhere
- Putting on make-up, fixing your hair, etc.
- Seeing old friends
- Going to office parties
- Going to concerts
- Friendly neighbors
- Criticizing someone
- Being popular at a gathering
- Pleasing others
- Belonging to a fraternity or sorority
- Debating
- Playing with pets
- Chatting on the internet
- Sending a SMS or MMS
- Getting new email
- Expressing love
- Being with family
- Being with friends
- Being told that you are loved
- Telling someone you love them
- Having a friend who truly believes in you
- Being told you are needed
- Making a difference in someone's life
- Encountering friends you haven't seen in a while

- Asking for help or advice
- Giving help or advice
- Being with happy people
- Being able to tell someone some good news
- Visiting people who are sick or in trouble
- Giving gifts
- Loaning something
- Coaching someone
- Doing favors for people
- Defending or protecting someone
- Having house guests
- Buying things for yourself
- Wearing new clothes
- Having a good relationship with your siblings
- Remembering someone
- Having friends you've known since your childhood
- Taking long talks with your friends about the past
- Finding and reading an old love letter
- Laughing at old family photos
- Spending time with someone you really like
- Being noticed as sexually attractive
- Being invited out
- Talking about sports
- Having a frank and open conversation
- Having a lively talk
- Shocking people
- Talking about sex
- Confessing or apologizing
- Telling people what to do
- Talking about politics or public affairs
- Talking about yourself
- Arguing
- Talking about your children or grandchildren
- Listening to someone else
- Playing with animals
- Going to a bar or club
- Going to church functions
- Talking with people on the job or in class

- Going to banquets, luncheons, potlucks, etc.
- Eating with friends or co-workers
- Going to a party
- Talking on the telephone
- Reuniting with loved ones
- Being able to count and trust someone
- Entertaining
- Getting a special message on your Facebook wall
- Getting real snail mail from someone special
- Being in love
- Sleeping next to someone you love
- Being at weddings, baptisms, graduations, etc.
- Going to a sports event
- Seeing a best friend you haven't seen in a long time
- Clicking with someone you just met
- Having eye contact
- Having best friends
- Catching the person you like looking at you
- Getting a phone call from someone you like
- Cheering someone on
- Hugging
- Complimenting someone
- Having someone agree with you
- Joining a club
- Shopping
- Smiling at people
- Having someone listen to you
- Watching people
- Feeling beautiful
- Being called beautiful
- Brushing your teeth
- Changing your hair color
- Getting your hair done
- Shaving
- Putting on perfume
- Witnessing a random act of kindness
- Thinking about other people's problems
- Talking about other people

ESCAPE/RELAXATION

- Listening to music
- Laughing
- Getting enough sleep
- Thinking about the past
- Going back to sleep in the morning
- Being right where you want to be
- Crying
- Knowing the words to a song
- Having some alone time
- Singing
- Dancing
- Dreaming
- Daydreaming
- Having nothing to do
- Hanging in sweats all day long
- Sitting in front of a fire
- Deep breathing
- Staying up late and sleeping late
- Going on vacation
- Laying on the grass and looking up at the sky
- Driving at night when no one is on the road
- Taking off your shoes
- Listening to live music
- Acting like a kid
- Having a television series marathon
- Playing and instrument
- Napping
- Getting something for free
- Getting away with something
- Gaining an hour of time
- Going on a picnic
- Getting on a plane, train or boat
- Getting something on sale
- Getting a parking spot
- Finding leftovers in the fridge

- Meditating
- Going downtown
- Praying
- Being in the country
- Going to the races (horse, car, boat, etc.)
- Reading stories, novels, poems, or plays
- Watching TV
- Camping
- Playing cards
- Driving long distances
- Exploring new places and things
- Watching animals
- Sitting and thinking
- Going to a fair, carnival, circus, or amusement park
- Talking about philosophy or religion
- Partying
- Watching the sky, clouds, or a storm
- Going on outings
- Being in the mountains
- Seeing beautiful scenery
- Having spare time
- Seeing famous people
- Going to the movies
- Having peace and quiet
- Relaxing
- Fantasizing
- Getting a massage
- Being outdoors
- Doing nothing
- Laughing
- Making a bucket list
- Having hobbies
- Eating
- Getting out of the house
- Gardening
- Going to a movie in the middle of the week
- Laying in the sun
- Doing yoga

- Walking in the woods or waterfront
- Sightseeing
- Having early morning coffee and newspaper
- Cooking
- Watching the sunrise or sunset
- Going to a restaurant
- Taking a long hot shower
- Taking a sauna or a steam bath
- Smelling flowers
- Soaking your feet in warm water, a pool, or a stream
- Whistling
- Traveling

PHYSICAL

- Taking a hot or cold shower or bath
- Driving or racing
- Going to a health club, sauna, bath, etc.
- Doing outdoor work
- Playing in sand, a stream, or the grass
- Feeling and hearing the wind
- Stretching
- Going naked
- Laying on a cold pillow
- Putting on warm clothes
- Having your muscles ache after a good workout
- Getting into a warm bed
- Drinking water when your thirsty
- Walking outside to the hot sun
- Walking inside when you have been out in the cold
- Dancing
- Putting socks on your cold feet
- Sitting in the sun
- Riding a motorcycle
- Swinging on a swing
- Cooking
- Preparing a new or special food
- Having coffee, tea, a coke, etc., with friends

- Eating snacks
- Listening to the sounds of nature
- Going on a roller coaster
- Taking a walk
- Doing something exciting such as rock climbing or parachuting
- Taking a walk in the early morning
- Kissing, petting or necking
- Having sex
- Looking at pornography
- Having a "butterflies in your stomach" kind of connection
- Breathing
- Doing sports
- Exercising
- Eating
- Masturbating
- Scratching
- Getting massages or backrubs
- Kicking leaves, sand, pebbles, etc.
- Giving massages or backrubs
- Walking barefoot
- Changing into clean and dry clothes
- Peeling layers of dried school glue off your hands
- Feeling the sunshine on your face
- Walking or running in the rain

MASTERY

- Working on your job
- Going to a business meeting or convention
- Canning, freezing, making preserves, etc.
- Going to school or government meetings
- Selling or trading something
- Repairing things
- Going to school reunions, alumni meetings, etc.
- Starting a new project
- Learning to do something new
- Completing a difficult task
- Paying bills

- Solving a problem, puzzle, crossword, etc.
- Giving a speech or lecture
- Reading maps
- Taking a class
- Learning a new language
- Advocating for something or someone
- Working on finances
- Making a major purchase or investment
- Getting a job promotion
- Winning a bet
- Writing papers, essays, articles, reports, memos, etc.
- Doing a job well
- Budgeting time
- Receiving recognition
- Planning your future
- Saving money
- Staying on a diet
- Doing experiments or other scientific work
- Playing board games
- Finishing a project or task
- Thinking about an interesting question
- Winning
- Teaching someone
- Doing volunteer work
- Going to a museum or exhibit
- Going to lectures or hearing speakers
- Solving a personal problem
- Reading the newspaper
- Going to the library
- Hearing a good sermon
- Being coached
- Surfing the Internet
- Doing art work
- Writing
- Making crafts
- Designing or drafting
- Getting an original idea
- Planning or organizing something

- Playing a musical instrument
- Reading
- Crossing things off your to-do list.
- Getting a really good grade
- Finishing way ahead of time
- Discovering a new shortcut
- Achieving something that you worked hard for
- Doing your best
- Winning
- Doing the right thing
- Conquering a fear

ENVIRONMENT

- Feeling the cold air of a fan or air conditioner
- Burning incense or scented candles
- Smelling fresh laundry
- Watching a fire
- Smelling food being cooked
- Seeing and being in a beautiful home
- Seeing or smelling a flower or plant
- Sitting in comfortable couch, chair, or bed
- Smelling fresh cut grass
- Seeing a big, bright, full moon
- Watching the clouds go by
- Being in nature
- Seeing or being in a beautifully lit home
- Smelling a BBQ
- Seeing flowers in the home
- Seeing and sitting in a beautiful set table
- Cleaning
- Seeing pictures on your walls
- Listening to nice music in the background
- Organizing
- Fixing things around the house
- Buying gadgets for the home
- Laying on clean sheets
- Painting the walls in your home
- Lighting candles

- Spraying air freshener around your home
- Organizing your closet
- Rearranging your home
- Caring for houseplants
- Seeing and being in a clean house

POSITIVITY

- Thinking about something good in the future
- Thinking about people you like or love
- Thinking about things for which you are thankful
- Thinking about pleasant events
- Finding positive reasons for why things happen
- Thinking you have things going for you
- Having thoughts about happy moments in childhood
- Remembering every detail of a beautiful day you had
- Thinking about the details of the beautiful day ahead
- Thinking about your good qualities
- Thinking that you will get what you want
- Thinking that the impossible is possible
- Thinking that you will overcome obstacles
- Thinking that you are worthy and valuable
- Thinking that the future is bright

NOTES

[1] Hill, R. (1996). The history of ethics. Retrieved from
http://www.coe.uga.edu/~rhill/workethic/hist.htm on 1/3/2011.

[2] Lyubomirsky, S., King, L., Diener, E. (2005). The benefits of
frequent positive affect: Does happiness lead to success?
Psychological Bulletin, 131(6), pp. 803-855.

[3] Schindler, J. (2002). *How to live 365 days a year*. PA: Running
Press Book Publishers.

[4] Maltz, M. (2001). The New *Psychocybernetics*. NY: Prentice Hall.

[5] Lyubomirsky, S., Sheldon, K., & Schkade, D. (2005). Pursuing
happiness: The architecture of sustainable change. *Review of
General Psychology*, Vol 9(2).

[6] Diener, E., Suh, M., Lucas, E., & Smith, H. (1999). Subjective well-
being: Three decades of progress. *Psychological Bulletin,* 125, 2,
276-302.

[7] Suh, E., Diener, E., Oishi, S., & Triandis, H. C. (1998). The shifting
of life satisfaction judgments across cultures: Emotions versus
norms. *Journal of Personality and Social Psychology, 74,* 482-
493.

[8] Aristotle, ., & Ostwald, M. (1962). *Nicomachean ethics*. ID: Bobbs-
Merrill.

[9] Retrieved from Merriam-Webster dictionary online www.merriam-
webster.com on 1/15/11.

[10] Lyubomirsky, King, & Diener op. cit.

[11] Braungart, J., Plomin, R., DeFries, J., & Fulker, D. (1992). Genetic
influence on tester-rated infant temperament as assessed by
Bayley's Infant Behavior Record: Nonadoptive and adoptive
siblings and twins. *Developmental Psychology, 28,* 40-47 as cited
in Diener et al. (1999).

[12] Lyubomirsky, S. (2008). *The how of happiness: A scientific
approach to getting the life you want*. NY: Penguin Press.

[13] Diener, E., & Lucas, R. E. (1999). Personality and subjective well-being. In D. Kahneman, E. Diener, & N. Schwartz (Eds.), *Well-being: The foundations of hedonic psychology* (pp. 213–229). Russell Sage Foundation: NY.

[14] Kahneman, D., Krueger, A., Schkade, D., Schwarz, N., & Stone, A. (2006). Would you be happier if you were richer? A focusing illusion. *Science*, 312(5782).

[15] Diener, Suh, Lucas & Smith, op. cit.

[16] Brickman, P., Coates, D., Janoff-Bulman, R. (1978). Lottery winners and accident victims: Is happiness relative? *Journal of Personality and Social Psychology*, 36, 917–927.

[17] Ibid.

[18] Silver, R. L. (1982). *Coping with an undesirable life event: A study of early reactions to physical disability*. Doctoral dissertation, Northwestern University, Evanston, IL.

[19] Mancini, A. D., Bonanno, G. A., & Clark, A. E. (2011). Stepping off the hedonic treadmill: Individual differences in response to major life events. *Journal of Individual Differences*, 32, 3, 144-152.

[20] Bonanno, G. A. (2004). Loss, trauma, and human resilience: Have we underestimated the human capacity to thrive after extremely aversive events? *The American Psychologist*, 59, 1, 20-8.

[21] Suh, E., Diener, E., & Fujita, F. (1996). Events and subjective well-being: Only recent events matter. *Journal of Personality and Social Psychology*, 70, 1091–1102.

[22] Lyubomirsky, King, & Diener op. cit.

[23] Ibid.

[24] Begley, 2007 as cited in Fredrickson, B. (2009). *Positivity*. NY: Crown Publishers.

[25] Ibid.

[26] Ilardi, S. S. (2010). *The depression cure: The 6-step program to beat depression without drugs*. MA: Da Capo Lifelong.

[27] Fordyce, M. (2000). *Human happiness: Its nature and its attainment*. Retrieved from www.gethappy.net on 10/31/10.

[28] Ibid.

[29] Sheldon, K., & Lyubomirsky, S. (2006). Achieving sustainable gains in happiness: Change your actions, not your circumstances. *Journal of Happiness Studies*, 7, 1, 55-86.

[30] Fordyce (2000), op. cit.

[31] Fordyce, M. W. (1983). A Program to increase happiness: Further studies. *Journal of Counseling Psychology, 30, 483-498.*

[32] Deci, E. & Ryan, R. (2006). Hedonia, eudaimonia, and well-being: An introduction. *Journal of Happiness Studies*, 9, 1-11.

[33] Kahneman, D., Diener, E., & Schwarz, N. (1999). *Well-being: The foundations of hedonic psychology.* NY: Russell Sage Foundation.

[34] Waterman, A. S. (1993). Two conceptions of happiness: Contrasts of personal expressiveness (eudaimonia) and hedonic enjoyment. *Journal of Personality and Social Psychology*, 64, 4, 678-691.

[35] Ibid.

[35] Ibid.

[36] Veenhoven, R. (2003). Hedonism and Happiness. *Journal of Happiness Studies*, 4, 4, 437-457.

[37] Kringelbach, M. L., & Berridge, K. C. (2010). *Pleasures of the brain.* Oxford: Oxford University Press.

[38] Cabanac, M. (2010). *Fifth influence: Or, the dialectics of pleasure.* S.l.: Iuniverse Inc.

[39] Ibid.

[40] Tugade & Fredrickson (2000) as cited in Fredrickson, B. L. (2001). The role of positive emotions in positive psychology. *The American Psychologist*, 56, 3, 218-26.

[41] Dillon, K. M., Minchoff, B., & Baker, K. H. (1985). Positive emotional states and enhancement of the immune system. *International Journal of Psychiatry in Medicine*, 15, 1, 1985-1986.

[42] Diener, E. & Diener, M. (1995). Cross-cultural correlates of life satisfaction and self-esteem. *Journal of Personality and Social Psychology* 68, pp. 653–663.

[43] Roysamb, E., Tambs, K., Reichborn-Kjennerud, T., Neale, M. C., & Harris, J. R. (2003). Happiness and health: Environmental and genetic contributions to the relationship between subjective well-being, perceived health, and somatic illness. *Journal of Personality and Social Psychology, 85,* 1136–1146.

[44] Danner, D. D., Snowdon, D. A., & Friesen, W. V. (2001). Positive emotions in early life and longevity: findings from the nun study. *Journal of Personality and Social Psychology*, 80, 5, 804-13.

[45] Ostir, G. V., Markides, K. S., Black, S. A., & Goodwin, J. S. (2000). Emotional well-being predicts subsequent functional independence and survival. *Journal of the American Geriatrics Society*, 48, 5, 473-8.

[46] Fordyce (2000), op. cit.

[47] Ryan, R. M., & Frederick, C. (1997). On energy, personality, and health: subjective vitality as a dynamic reflection of well-being. *Journal of Personality*, 65, 3, 529-65.

[48] Bloom, W. (2001). *The endorphin effect: A breakthrough strategy for holistic health and spiritual wellbeing.* UK: Judy Piaktus.

[49] Fuhrman, J. (2003). *Eat to Live.* Little, Brown and Company: NY.

[50] Fordyce (2000), op. cit.

[51] Fredrickson, B. L. (2001). The role of positive emotions in positive psychology. The broaden-and-build theory of positive emotions. *The American Psychologist*, 56, 3, 218-26.
Lyubomirsky, op. cit.

[52] Fordyce (2000), op. cit.

[53] Ibid.

[54] Ibid.

[55] Ibid.

[56] Derryberry, D., & Tucker, D. M. (1994). Motivating the focus of attention. In P. M. Neidenthal & S. Kitayama (Eds.), *The heart's eye: Emotional influences in perception and attention* (pp. 167-196). CA: Academic Press.

[57] Fordyce (2000), op. cit.

[58] Ibid.

[59] Ibid.

[60] Wallenstein, G. (2009). The Pleasure Instinct: *Why we crave adventure, chocolate, pheromones, and music.* NJ: Wiley & Sons.

[61] Ryan, R. L., & Deci, E. L. (2000). Self-determination theory and the facilitation of intrinsic motivation, social development, and well-being. *American Psychologist, 55,* 68-78.

[62] Fredrickson, B. L., & Branigan, C. (2001). Positive emotions. In T. J. Mayne & G. A. Bonnano (Eds.), *Emotion: Current issues and future directions* (pp. 123-151). NY: Guilford Press.

[63] Csikszentmihalyi, M. (1990). *Flow: The psychology of optimal experience.* NY: Harper Perennial.

[64] Fordyce (2000), op. cit.

[65] Ibid.

[66] Csikszentmihalyi, M., & Wong, M. M. (1991). The situational and personal correlates of happiness: A cross-national comparison. In F. Strack, M. Argyle, & N. Schwarz (Eds.), *Subjective well-being: An interdisciplinary perspective* (pp. 193–212). NY: Pergamon Press.

[67] Ryff, C. D. (1989). Happiness is everything, or is it? Explorations on the meaning of psychological well-being. *Journal of Personality and Social Psychology, 57*, 1069–1081.

[68] Fordyce (2000), op. cit.

[69] Weiss, H. M., Nicholas, J. P., & Daus, C. S. (1999). An examination of the joint effects of affective experiences and job beliefs on job satisfaction and variations in affective experiences over time. *Organizational Behavior and Human Decision Processes, 78*, 1–24.

[70] Campbell, Converse & Rogers (1976) as cited in Lyubomirsky, King & Diener op. cit.

[71] Fordyce (2000), op. cit.

[72] Lyubomirsky, Sheldon & Schkade, op. cit.

[73] Ibid.

[74] Ibid.

[75] Ibid.

[76] Tarlow, E. M., & Haaga, D. A. F. (1996). Negative self-concept: Specificity to depressive symptoms and relation to positive and negative affectivity. *Journal of Research in Personality, 30*, 120–127.

[77] Fordyce (2000), op. cit.

[78] Diener, E., & Seligman, M. E. P. (2002). Very happy people. *Psychological Science, 13*, 81–84.

[79] Fordyce (2000), op. cit.

[80] Fredrickson, B. L. (2001). The role of positive emotions in positive psychology. The broaden-and-build theory of positive emotions. *The American Psychologist*, 56, 3, 218-26.

[81] Bogner, Corrigan, Mysiw, Clinchot, & Fugate (2001) as cited in Lyubomirsky, King & Diener.

[82] Fredrickson, op. cit.

[83] Ibid.

[84] Lyubomirsky, King & Diener, op. cit.

[85] Ibid.

[86] Orezeck, McGuire & Longnecker (1958) as cited in Fordyce (2000), op. cit.

[87] Wessman, & Ricks (1966) as cited in Fordyce (2000), op. cit.

[88] Fredrickson, op. cit.

[89] Ibid.

[90] Krueger, Hicks, & McGue (2001) as cited in Lyubomirsky, King & Diener, op. cit.

[91] Williams, S., & Shiaw, W. (1999). Mood and organizational citizenship behavior: The effects of positive affect on employee. *Journal of Psychology*, 133(6), 656.

[92] Brock & Becker (1967) as cited in Fordyce (2000), op. cit.

[93] Maslow (1962) as cited in Fordyce (2000), op. cit.

[94] Bradburn & Caplovitz (1965) as cited in Fordyce (2000), op. cit.

[95] Wessman, op. cit.

[96] Bradburn, op. cit.

[97] Wessman, op. cit.

[98] Ibid.

[99] Hersey (1932) as cited in Fordyce (2000), op. cit.

[100] Connolly & Viswesvaran, 2000 as cited in Lyubomirsky, King & Diener, op. cit.

[101] Sherman (1971) as cited in Fordyce (2000), op. cit.

[102] Wright & Staw (1999) as cited in Lyubomirsky, King, & Diener, op. cit.

[103] Staw, Sutton, & Pelled, 1994 as cited in Lyubomirsky, King, & Diener, op. cit.

[104] Frisch et al., 2004 as cited in Lyubomirsky, King, & Diener, op. cit.

[105] Veenhoven, op. cit.

[106] Oishi, op. cit.

[107] Frijda, op. cit.

[108] Bloom, op. cit.

[109] Cabanac, M. (2010). *Fifth influence: Or, the dialectics of pleasure.* S.l.: Iuniverse Inc.

[110] Frijda, N. (2010). On the nature and function of pleasure. In M.L. Kringelbach and K.C. Berridge (Eds.) *Pleasures of the brain*, pp.99-112. NY: Oxford University Press.

[111] Schooler, J. & Mauss, I. (2010). To be happy and to know it. In M.L. Kringelbach and K.C. Berridge (Eds.) *Pleasures of the brain*, pp.99-112. NY: Oxford University Press.

[112] Schooler & Mauss, op. cit.

[113] Frijda, op. cit.

[114] Kringelbach, M. L., & Berridge, K. C. (2010). *Pleasures of the brain*. Oxford: Oxford University Press.

[115] Cabanac, op. cit.

[116] Oishi, S., Schimmack, U., & Diener, E. (2001). Pleasures and subjective well-being. *European Journal of Personality*, 15, 153-167.

[117] Fordyce (2000), op. cit.

[118] Gladwell, M. (2006). *Malcolm Gladwell on spaghetti sauce*. TED Ideas Worth Spreading. Retrieved from http://www.ted.com/talks/malcolm_gladwell_on_spaghetti_sauce.html on 12/12/10.

[119] Berns, G. (2005). *Satisfaction: The science of finding true fulfillment*. NY: Holt & Co.

[120] Fordyce (2000), op. cit.

[121] Lyubomirsky, 2008, op. cit.

[122] Tkach, C., & Lyubomirsky, S. (2006). How do people pursue happiness? Relating personality, happiness-increasing strategies, and well-being. *Journal of Happiness Studies*, 7, 2, 183-225.

[123] Lewinsohn, P. (n.d.). *Pleasant events schedule*. Retrieved from http://www.healthnetsolutions.com/dsp/PleasantEventsSchedule.pdf on 5/1/10.

[124] Fordyce (2000), op. cit.

Csikszentmihalyi, M. & Hunter, J. (2003). Happiness in Everyday Life: The Use of Experience Sampling. *Journal of Happiness Studies* 4, pp. 185–199.

Tkach & Lyubomirsky, op. cit.

[125] Baumeisl:er, R. F.. & Leary, M. R. (1995). The need to belong: Desire for interpersonal attachment as a fundamental human motivation. *Psychological Bulletin, 117,*497-529.

[126] Ornish, D. (1998). *Love and survival: The scientific basis for the healing power of intimacy*. NY: Harper Collins

[127] Rumsey, N. (2008). The psychology of appearance: Why health psychologists should "do looks". *The European Health*

Psychologist, Vol 10. Retrieved from
http://hls.uwe.ac.uk/research/Data/Sites/1/docs/CAR/EHP_Sept_2
008_NRumsey.pdf on 10/7/10.

[128] Ryan & Deci op. cit.

[129] Langlois J.H., Kalakanis L., Rubenstein AJ., Larson A., Hallam
M., Smoot M. (2000). Maxims or myths of beauty? A meta-
analytic and theoretical review. *Psychol. Bull.* 126:390–423

[130] Feingold, A. (1992). Gender differences in mate selection
preferences: a test of the parental investment model.
Psychological Bulletin, 112, 1, 125-39.

[131] Langlois, op. cit.

[132] Ibid.

[133] Ornish, op. cit

[134] Keegan, L. (January 01, 2003). Therapies to reduce stress and
anxiety. *Critical Care Nursing Clinics of North America*, 15, 3,
321-7.

[135] Willert, M., Thulstrup, A., Hertz, J., Bonde, J. (2010). Sleep and
cognitive failures improved by a three-month stress management
intervention. *International Journal of Stress Management*, 17(3),
193-213.

[136] Hamilton, N., Nelson, C., Stevens, N., & Kitzman, H. (2007).
Sleep and psychological well-being. *Social Indicators Research*,
82 (1), 147-163.

[137] Woynarowski, D. (n.d.). *Discover why sleep deprivation is a silent
killer and the all natural solutions you can use to sleep well
tonight.* Transcript of exclusive interview with Dr. Dave
Woynarowski. Retrieved from
http://www.drdavesbest.com/downloads/Sleep_Interview_Transcr
ipt.pdf on 11/4/10.

[138] Akerstedt, T. (2006). Psychosocial stress and impaired sleep.
Scandinavian Journal of Work, Environment & Health, 32, 6,
493-501.

[139] Meditation Oasis. *Difficulty meditating. Keys to easy, effortless
meditation...* Retrieved from
http://www.meditationoasis.com/how-to-meditate/difficulty-
meditating/on 4/4/11.

[140] Retrieved from
http://answers.yahoo.com/question/index?qid=20090723202429A
AyD7o on 4/7/11.

[141] Retrieved from
http://answers.yahoo.com/question/index?qid=20090723202429A
AyD7o on 4/7/11

[142] Lutz, A., Slagter, H., Dunne, J., Davidson, R. (2008). Attention
regulation and monitoring in meditation. *Trends in Cognitive
Sciences*, vol. xxx, no. x. Retrieved from
http://brainimaging.waisman.wisc.edu/~lutz/Lutz_attention_regul
ation_monitoring_meditation_tics_2008.pdf on 3/2/11.

[143] Cass, H. & Holford, P. (2002). *Natural highs: supplements,
nutrition, and mind-body techniques to help you feel good all the
time.* NY: Penguin.

[144] Bloomfield, H. & Kory, R. (1976). *Happiness: The TM program,
psychiatry, and enlightment.* NY: Dawn Press.

[145] Hoppock (1935) as cited in Fordyce (2000), op. cit.

[146] Wilson (1960) as cited in Fordyce (2000), op. cit.

[147] Martin, R. A. (January 01, 2001). Humor, laughter, and physical
health: methodological issues and research findings.
Psychological Bulletin, 127, 4, 504-19.

[148] Dixon, N. (1980). Humor: A cognitive alternative to stress. In
Spielberger, C. D. and I. G. Sarason (eds.), *Anxiety and Stress*,
Vol. 7, 281–289.

[149] Ibid.

[150] Ibid.

[151] Martin, R. A., & Lefcourt, H. M. (1983). Sense of humor as a
moderator of the relation between stressors and moods. *Journal of
Personality and Social Psychology*, 45 (6), 1313-1324.

[152] Martin, R. & Dobbin, J. (1988). Sense of humor, hassles, and
immunoglobulin A: Evidence for a stress-moderating effect of
humor. *The International Journal of Psychiatry in Medicine*,
18(2), 93-105.

[153] *Theory and guidelines for therapists (n.d.).* Retrieved from
http://Cinematherapy.com/theory.html on 11/2/10.

[154] Marrs, R. W. (1995). A meta-analysis of bibliotherapy studies.
American Journal of Community Psychology, 23(6), 843- 870.

[155] Brown, E. F. (1975). *Bibliotherapy and its' widening applications.* NJ: Scarecrow Press, Inc.

[156] Wikipedia. *Synchronicity.* Retrieved from http://en.wikipedia.org/wiki/Synchronicity on 1/3/11.

[157] North, C. & Glaser, S. (1997*). Synchronicity: The anatomy of coincidence.* CA: Regent Press.

[158] Lyubomirsky, S., & Tucker, K. L. (1998). Implications of individual differences in subjective happiness for perceiving, interpreting, and thinking about life events. *Motivation and Emotion, 22,* 155-186.

[159] Tkach & Lyubomirsky, op. cit.

[160] Cowan, Neighbors, DeLaMoreaux, & Behnke, 1998 as cited in Fredrickson, B. (2009). *Positivity.* New York: Crown Publishers.

[161] Pfeiffer & Wong (1989) as cited in Fredrickson, 2009, op. cit.

[162] Fredrickson, 2008, op. cit.

[163] Folkman, S., & Moskowitz, J. T. (2000). Positive affect and the other side of coping. *The American Psychologist*, 55, 6, 647-54.

[164] Emmons, R. A., & McCullough, M. E. (2003). Counting blessings versus burdens: an experimental investigation of gratitude and subjective well-being in daily life. *Journal of Personality and Social Psychology*, 84, 2, 377-89.

[165] Field, T. (2011). Touch for socio-emotional and physical well-being: A review. *Developmental Review*, 30(4), 367-383.

[166] Ibid.

[167] Cass & Holford, op. cit.

[168] Field, op. cit.

[169] Ibid.

[170] Cass & Holford, op. cit.

[171] Carey, B. (2010). Evidence that little touches do mean so much. *The New York Times*. Retrieved from http://www.nytimes.com/2010/02/23/health/23mind.html on 3/11/11.

[172] *Rocking Chair Therapy.* Retrieved from http://www.rockingchairtherapy.org/research.html on 3/3/11.

[173] Medical Research. *The floating bed.* Retrieved from http://www.floatingbed.com/features-benefits/medical-research/ on 4/5/11.

[174] *Rocking motion.* Retrieved from http://www.designboom.com/history/rockingmotion.html on 3/11/11.

[175] Ibid.

[176] Shaver & Freedman (1976) as cited in Fordyce (2000), op. cit.

[177] Ibid.

[178] Brock (1965) as cited in Fordyce (2000), op. cit.

[179] Wilson (1960) as cited in Fordyce (2000), op. cit.

[180] Blanchflower, D. G., & Oswald, A. J. (2004). Money, Sex and Happiness: An Empirical Study. The *Scandinavian Journal of Economics*, 106, 3, 393-415.

[181] Fordyce, op. cit.

[182] Sailer (1931) as cited in Fordyce (2000), op. cit.

[183] Ornstein, R. and Sobel, D. (1989). *Healthy Pleasures*. Reading: Addison- Wesley.

[184] Ilardi, op. cit.

[185] Ibid.

[186] Stubbe, J., de Moor, M., Boomsma, D., de Geus, E.,(2007). The association between exercise participation and well-being: A co-twin study. *Preventive Medicine*, 44(2), 148-152

[187] Blumenthal, J. A., Babyak, M. A., Doraiswamy, P. M., Watkins, L., Hoffman, B. M., Barbour, K. A., Herman, S., & Sherwood, A. (2007). Exercise and pharmacotherapy in the treatment of major depressive disorder. *Psychosomatic Medicine*, 69, (7).

[188] North, T. C, McCullagh, P., & Tran, Z. V. (1990). Effect of exercise on depression. *Exercise and Sport Science Review, 18*, 379-415.

[189] Lawlor, D. A., & Hopker, S. W. (2001). The effectiveness of exercise as an intervention in the management of depression: systematic review and meta-regression analysis of randomized controlled trials. *British Medical Journal*, 322, 7289, 763-766.

[190] Ilardi, op. cit.

[191] Cass & Holford, op. cit.

[192] Cason (1931) from Fordyce (2000), op. cit.

[193] Cantril (1965) from Fordyce (2000), op. cit.

[194] Thayer, R. E., Newman, J. R., & McClain, T. M. (1994). Self-regulation of mood: Strategies for changing a bad mood, raising energy, and reducing tension. *Journal of Personality and Social*

Psychology, 67,910–925.

[195] American Psychological Association (2006). *Americans engage in unhealthy behaviors to manage stress*. Retrieved from http://www.apa.org/news/press/releases/2006/01/stress-management.aspx on 5/4/11.

[196] Berns (2005), op. cit.

[197] *Mindfulness exercises (n.d.)*. Retrieved from www.dbtcentermi.org/uploads/Mindfulness_Exercises.doc on 3/28/11.

[198] *Tasting deeply (n.d.)*. Retrieved from www.mindfuleating.org/TastingDeeply.html on 5/4/11.

[199] Gorman, 1971 cited from Veenhoven, op. cit.

[200] Zuckerman, M. (1990). The psychophysiology of sensation seeking. *Journal of Personality*, 58 (1), 313-45.

[201] Reisenzein, R. (1994). Pleasure-arousal theory and the intensity of emotions. *Journal of Personality and Social Psychology*, 67, 3, 525-539.

[202] Berns, op. cit.

[203] Berns, op. cit.

[204] Zuckerman, op. cit.

[205] Ibid.
Donohew, L., Zimmerman, R., Cupp, P. S., Novak, S., Colon, S., & Abell, R. (2000). Sensation seeking, impulsive decision-making, and risky sex: implications for risk-taking and design of interventions. *Personality and Individual Differences*, 28 (6), 1079-1091.

[206] Zuckerman, M. (1994). *Behavioral expressions and biosocial bases of sensation seeking*. MA: Cambridge University Press.

[207] Berne, 1951 cited from Steiner, C. (n.d.). *Transactional analysis in the information age*. Retrieved from http://www.claudesteiner.com/tainfo.htm on 1/1/11.

[208] Zuckerman, op. cit.

[209] Pickering, A. D. (2004). The neuropsychology of impulsive antisocial sensation seeking personality traits: From dopamine to hippocampal function. In R. M. Stelmack (Ed.), *On the psychobiology of personality: Essays in honor of Marvin Zuckerman* (pp. 454–476). NY: Elsevier.

[210] Fulker, D. W., Eysenck, S. B. G., & Zuckerman, M. (1980). A genetic and environmental analysis of sensation seeking. *Journal of Research in Personality*, 14, 261–281.

[211] Jackson, 2005 cited from Jackson, C. J. (2009). *Using the hybrid model of learning in personality to predict performance in the workplace*. 8th IOP Conference, Conference Proceedings, Manly, Sydney, Australia.

[212] George L. (1992). *Mastery: The keys to success and long-term fulfillment*. NY: Penguin.

[213] Csikszentmihalyi, op. cit.

[214] Hennessey, B. A. (1999). Intrinsic motivation, affect and creativity. In S. Russ (Ed.), *Affect, Creative Experience and Psychological Adjustment*. PA: Taylor & Francis.

[215] Runco M.A. (1999). Time for Creativity. In Runco and Pritzker (Eds.) 1999, *Encyclopedia of Creativity*. CA: Academic.

[216] Barron, F. X. (1963). *Creativity and Psychological Health: Origins of Personal Vitality and Creative Freedom*. NJ: Van Nostrand.

[217] Ulirch, R., Zimring, C., Quan, X. et. Al. (2006). The environment's impact on stress. In S. Marberry (Eds.), *Improving healthcare with better building design*. IL: Health Administration Press.

[218] Ulrich, R. (1984). View through a window may influence recovery from surgery. *Science*, 224: 420-21.

[219] Ulrich, R. (1991). Effects of interior design on wellness: Theory and recent scientific research. *Journal of Health Care Interior Design*, 3, 97-109.

[220] Ulrich, R. S. (1983). Aesthetic and affective response to natural environment. In I. Altman & J. F. Wohlwill, (Eds.), *Human Behavior and Environment*. NY: Plenum Press.

[221] Korpela, K. M., & Ylén, M. P. (2009). Effectiveness of Favorite-Place Prescriptions. *American Journal of Preventive Medicine*, 36, 5, 435.

[222] Zeisel, J. Silverstein N., Hyde, J. et. Al. (2003). Environmental correlates to behavioral outcomes in Alzheimer's special care units. *The Gerontologist*, 43, 697-711.

[223] Benedetti et. Al. (2001). Morning sunlight reduces length of hospitalizations in bipolar depression. *Journal of Affective Disorders*, 62: 221-23.

[224] Ulrich, R. (1984), op. cit.

[225] Ulrich, R. S. and Zimring, C., Quan, X., Joseph, A., Choudhary, R. (2004). *The Role of the Physical Environment in the Hospital of the 21st Century.* The Center for Health Design and the Robert Wood Johnson Foundation. Retrieved from www.healthdesign.org on 12/4/10.

[226] Ulrich, 1991, op. cit.

[227] Berger, R. & McLeod, J. (2006). Incorporating Nature Into Therapy: A Framework For Practice. *Journal of Systemic Therapies,* 25(2), 80-94.

[228] Van den Berg, A.E. (2005) *Health impacts of healing environments: A review of the benefits of nature, daylight, fresh air and quiet in healthcare settings.* Groningen: Foundation 200 years University Hospital Groningen.

[229] Ulrich, R. (1999). Effects of gardens on health outcomes: Theory and research. Cooper Marcus & Barnes (Eds.), *Healing Gardens.* NY: Wiley.

[230] Frumkin, H. (2001) Beyond toxicity human: health and the natural environment. *American Journal of Preventative Medicine,* 20, 234.

[231] Berger, R., & McLeod, J. (2006). Incorporating nature into therapy: A framework for practice. *Journal of Systemic Therapies,* 25 (2), 80-94.

[232] Kinder, D. W. (2002). *Nature and psyche: Radical environmentalism and the politics of subjectivity.* NY: State University of New York.

[233] Golden, R. N., Gaynes, B. N., Ekstrom, R. D., Hamer, R. M., Jacobsen, F. M., Suppes, T., Wisner, K. L., & Nemeroff, C. B. (2005). The efficacy of light therapy in the treatment of mood disorders: a review and meta-analysis of the evidence. *The American Journal of Psychiatry,* 162 (4), 656-62.

[234] Ilardi, op. cit.

[235] Fredrickson, B. (2009). *Positivity.* NY: Crown Publishers.

[236] Van den Berg, op. cit.

[237] Takeda, H., Tsujita, J., Kaya, M., Takemura, M., & Oku, Y. (2008). Differences between the physiologic and psychological effects of aromatherapy body treatment. *The Journal of Alternative and Complementary Medicine,* 14(6), 655–661.

[238] Herz, R. S. (2009). Aromatherapy facts and fictions: A scientific

analysis of olfactory effects on mood, physiology and behavior. *International Journal of Neuroscience*, 119, 2, 263-290.

[239] Morrison, W. Hass, E., Shaffner, D. (2003). Noise, stress, and annoyance in a pediatric intensive care unit. *Critical Care Medicine*, 31, 113-119.

[240] Hays T. (2006). Facilitating well-being through music for older people. *Home Health Care Services Quarterly*, 25(374), 55-73.

[241] Laukka, P. (2007). Uses of music and psychological well-being among the elderly. *Journal of Happiness Studies, 8*, 215-241.

[242] Lai, H.L., & Good, M. (2006). 30th ANNIVERSARY ISSUE: Music improves sleep quality in older adults. *Journal of Advanced Nursing*, 53 (1), 134-144.

[243] Retrieved from http://thinkexist.com/quotation/some_pursue_happiness-others_create_it/154636.html on 6/5/11.

[244] Fordyce (2000), op. cit

[245] Lyubomirsky, (2008), p. 23, op. cit.

[246] Brown, K., Ryan, R., Creswell, D., (2007). Mindfulness: theoretical foundations and evidence for its salutary effects. *Psychological Inquiry, 18* (4), 211-237

[247] Kabat-Zinn, J. (2005). *Coming to Our Senses: Healing Ourselves and The World through Mindfulness*. NY: Hyperion Books.

[248] Knaster, M. (1996). *Discovering the Body's Wisdom*. CA: Bantam New Age Books.

[249] Adult Pleasant Events Schedule (n.d.). Retrieved from http://www.dbtselfhelp.com/html/er_handout_8.html on 1/2/11.

Pleasurable activities (n.d.). Retrieved from http://www.depressioncenter.org/MDOCC/pdf/SM%20Activity-Pleasurable%20Activities.pdf on 1/2/11.

McKay, M., Wood, J., Brandley, J. (2007). Dialectical Behavior Therapy Skills Workbook: Practical DBT Exercises for Learning Mindfulness, Interpersonal Effectiveness, Emotion Regulation, & Distress Tolerance. CA: New Harbinger Publications, Inc.

Lewinsohn, P. (n.d.). Pleasant Events Schedule. Retrieved from http://www.healthnetsolutions.com/dsp/PleasantEventsSchedule.pdf

Mahaney, E. (n.d.). Pleasurable Activities List. Retrieved from http://www.southtampatherapy.com/South_Tampa_Therapy/Eliza

beths_Blog/Entries/2009/1/3_Pleasurable_Activities_List.html on 1/1/11.

List of Pleasurable Activities (n.d.). Retrieved from http://www.counselingexcellence.com/Josh_Mark/Free%20Stuff%20&%20Tools_files/List%20Of%20Pleasurable%20Activities.pdf on 1/1/11.

Roane, S. (n.d.). The Big List of Pleasurable Activities. Retrieved from http://www.urbanbalance.org/Urban-Balance-Blog/ub-counseling-info-for-chicago-therapy.html on 1/1/11.

Pleasurable Activities to Choose From (n.d.). Retrieved from http://drsgoldstein.com/Documents/183%20Pleasurable%20Activities%20to%20Choose%20From.pdf on 1/1/11.

Pleasant Activities List (n.d.). Retrieved from http://www.raleighpsychology.com/pleasant.htm on 1/1//11.

ABOUT THE AUTHOR

Marisol Garcia is a therapist, social researcher, writer, and lecturer. She received her doctorate from the University of Connecticut. Her private practice is located in Orange, Connecticut and New York City. Marisol is Assistant Director for Partners in Social Research. To learn more about her work, you can visit her website at www.garciawestberg.com.

58479885R00086

Made in the USA
Middletown, DE
06 August 2019